FRANK & POLLY MUIR'S BIG DIPPER

A book of specially written and drawn stories,
poems, articles and pictures, designed to give
pleasure to children, parents, grandparents
—and everybody else—who Dips In.

HEINEMANN : LONDON

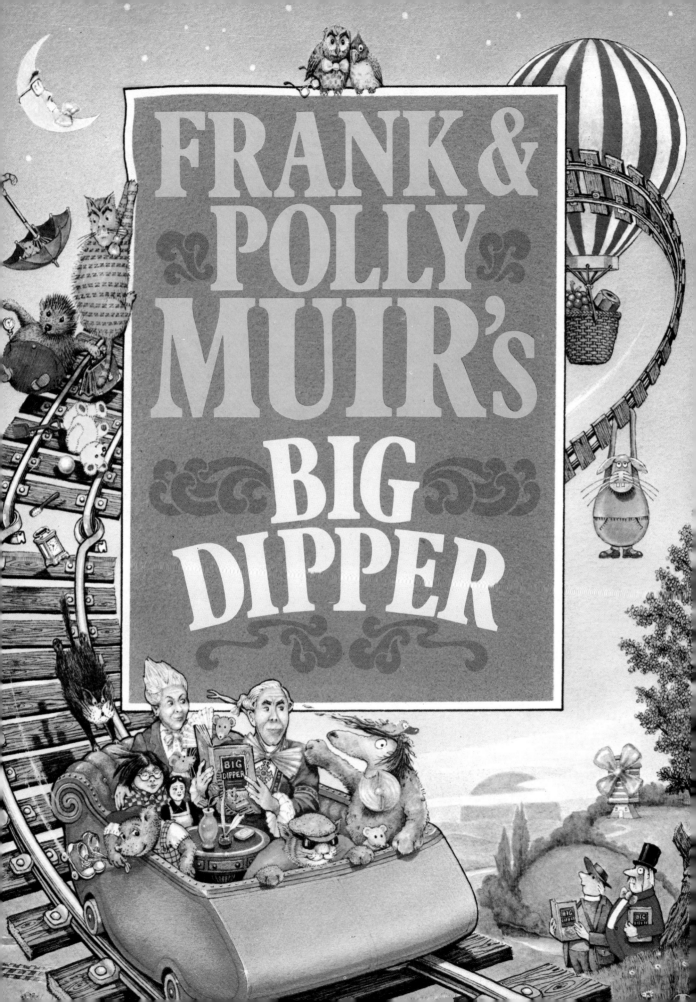

FRANK & POLLY MUIR'S

BIG DIPPER

Designed by Craig Dodd

Cover, half-title and title page illustration by

Peter Cross

First published 1981
Compilation © Frank Muir Limited 1981

434 95170 6
Phototypeset by Tradespools Limited, Frome, Somerset
Printed in Italy

William Heinemann Ltd
10 Upper Grosvenor Street, London W1X 9PA
LONDON MELBOURNE TORONTO
JOHANNESBURG AUCKLAND

Frank Muir

Anners · Thorpe · Egham · Surrey · TW20 8UE · Chertsey 62759

Dear Reader (and you qualify as a reader if you have got this far),

A word about this book, to help you if you are deciding whether to buy it or not, or are wondering whether to take it out of the library, or have been given it and do not know what it is.

It is a collection of specially commissioned pieces and pictures meant for the whole family. We have tried to bring together not only examples of the work of our very best writers and illustrators of children's books but also pieces which we particularly like from writers and artists who are just beginning to do this sort of work. We have also persuaded some friends of ours, who are distinguished in other fields but have never written or drawn for children before, to try their hand at this demanding and difficult work.

Quite a lot of the pieces are funny but not all. A few are more thoughtful. There are also jokes, cartoons, poems, and one or two pictures which are just meant to be looked at. It is a book for you to Dip Into. Our hope is that you will begin by reading the sort of thing that you know that you like but will then go on to discover a whole new range of pleasures.

When you discover new writers and artists and want to see more of their work you can turn to the back of the book where we give details of what other books they have written and who publishes them.

So, turn to the list of contents over the page, see whether your favourite authors and illustrators are there or whether they are all favourites-to-be, and away you go.

Good Dipping!

Frank + *Polly Muir*

Contents

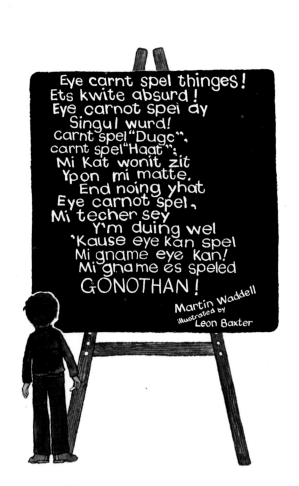

Eye carnt spel thinges!
Ets kwite absurd!
Eye carnot spel áy
Singul wurd!
Carnt spel "Dugc",
carnt spel "Haat";
Mi Kat wonit zit
Ypon mi matte.
End noing yhat
Eye carnot spel,
Mi techer sey
Y'm duing wel
'Kause eye kan spel
Mi gname eye kan!
Mi gname es speled
GONOTHAN!

Martin Waddell
Illustrated by
Leon Baxter

BRUNO the BEAR in ROLLER BEAR

BY COLIN McNAUGHTON

TAKING A DIFFERENT ROUTE HOME FROM SCHOOL ONE AFTERNOON BRUNO CAME ACROSS A VERY INTERESTING SIGHT.

WHERE THE OLD BINGO HALL SIGN SHOULD HAVE BEEN WAS NOW A DAZZLING NEW SIGN...

RINKI·DINKI·DOODLE·ROLLER·SKATING·RINK
The Latest and the Greatest

Hello, this is new — it used to be a Bingo hall

HE LOOKED IN THE WINDOW

AND THIS IS WHAT HE SAW

whizz

Yahoo

weeee

zoom

IT WAS THE MOST EXCITING THING HE HAD EVER SEEN!

It's the most exciting thing I've ever seen!

NEXT DOOR TO THE RINK BRUNO FOUND A SPORTS SHOP SELLING AMAZING ROLLER SKATES

9

BRUNO WANDERED HOME DEEP IN THOUGHT

HE RAIDED HIS MONEY BOX...

...HE ASKED HIS DAD...

. HE FOUND A JOB DELIVERING NEWSPAPERS...

...HE RAN ERRANDS...

...HE MOWED LAWNS...

...HE CUT HEDGES...

...HE SOLD HIS BIKE...

...HE EVEN WENT TO SEE HIS RICH AUNT MIMI!

AT LAST HE HAD ENOUGH MONEY FOR HIS SKATES.

IT WASN'T AS EASY AS IT LOOKED

It's not as easy as it looks

BUT BRUNO WASN'T GOING TO GIVE UP. NOT AFTER ALL THE TROUBLE HE HAD BEEN THROUGH TO BUY HIS SKATES. SO, EVERY NIGHT AFTER SCHOOL AND AT WEEKENDS, HE PRACTISED ROLLER SKATING.

Wo-o-o-o-a-a-a-a-r-r-R-G-G-H-H-H-O-O-O-O-O-F-F-F-F

SLOWLY, BUT SURELY

WITH THE ODD SETBACK

HE GOT BETTER,

weeee

AND BETTER.

whizz

THEY DO SAY 'PRACTICE MAKES PERFECT'

Practice Makes Perfect

YAHOO!

Rinki Dinki Doodle Roller Skating Rink here I come!

ZOOM

THE DAY CAME WHEN...

ZOOM

...BRUNO WAS READY!

Is it a plane?

Is it a bird?

NO! IT'S ROLLER BEAR

Whizzz

BUT WHEN HE ARRIVED-HE STOPPED IN HORROR!

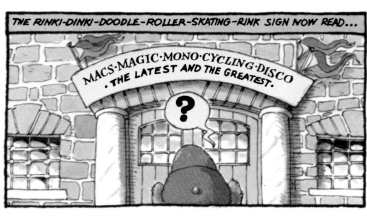

THE RINKI-DINKI-DOODLE-ROLLER-SKATING-RINK SIGN NOW READ...

MACS·MAGIC·MONO·CYCLING·DISCO
·THE LATEST AND THE GREATEST·

?

HE CROSSED THE STREET

AND LOOKED IN THE WINDOW

AND THIS IS WHAT HE SAW!

whizzz

wahoo

IT WAS THE MOST EXCITING THING HE HAD EVER SEEN

It's the most exciting thing I've ever seen

NEXT DOOR TO 'MACS MAGIC MONO-CYCLING DISCO, IN THE SPORTS SHOP WHERE BRUNO HAD BOUGHT HIS ROLLER SKATES, THEY WERE NOW SELLING THE MOST AMAZING MONO-CYCLES...

I've just got to have one of those mono-cycles. But how?

HERE WE GO AGAIN!

The End?

Penelope Lively
UNINVITED GHOSTS
Illustrated by
Kate Penoyre

When the Browns moved to their new house they left the old one empty. The rooms were swept and bare. The windows had no curtains. The walls had pale squares where the pictures had been.

The new house was like that, too. It seemed quite empty. The Browns spent a dreadful day moving in. It was all fuss and bustle. Mrs Brown broke her best teapot. Mr Brown fell off a ladder. Simon (who was eight) put his foot through the bathroom floor. Marian (who was nine) lost her pencil set. The cat took one look and ran away.

A chest of drawers and two removal men got stuck on the stairs for half an hour.

At last, it was all done, and everybody was in a bad temper with everybody else. There was nothing but bread and margarine for supper. The cat came back and was sick on the kitchen floor. The television wouldn't work and the children were sent to bed.

It was then that they found the house was not empty.

First, Marian put her jersey in a drawer. She banged the drawer shut and a voice said "Ouch!"

Marian said to Simon, "I never touched you, stupid."

Simon said, "Stupid yourself!"

They were just about to get down to a proper battle, since both of them were tired and cross, when something else happened.

The drawer slid slowly open, and out came a pale grey shape, about three feet high, smelling of woodsmoke. It sat down on a chair and began to hum to itself. It looked like a bundle of bedclothes, except that it was not solid. You could see, quite clearly, the cushion on the chair underneath it.

Marian took one huge jump into bed and shrieked, "That's a ghost!"

The ghost said, "It's not nice to call people names. Be quiet and go to sleep."

It climbed on to the end of Simon's bed, took out a ball of wool and some needles and began to knit.

Have you ever tried telling your mother that you can't get to sleep because there is a ghost sitting on the end of your bed, clacking its knitting-needles? I shouldn't. She would probably say the sort of things that Mrs Brown said to Simon.

The trouble was, the ghost only appeared to Simon and Marian. "I like children," it said cosily, "always have. Eat up your dinner, there's a good boy." At this point it was sitting on the kitchen table, breathing down Simon's neck.

They couldn't get away from it. When they were watching television it sat itself down between them and talked loudly through all the best bits. When they wouldn't answer it poked them in the ribs. That was like being nudged by a damp, cold cloud. It trailed round the garden after them when they were playing. It made remarks when they were trying to do their homework. "Now then," it would say sternly, "no looking out of the window. No chewing the end of your pencil. When *I* was your age . . ."

"Go *away*, can't you!" yelled Simon. "This is our house now."

"No, it isn't," said the ghost smugly. "Always been here, I have. A hundred years or more. Seen plenty of families come and go, I have."

At the end of the first week the children woke up to find the ghost sitting on the wardrobe reading a newspaper. The newspaper had the date 1871 on it. The ghost was smoking a long white clay pipe.

Beside it there was a second grey, cloudy shape.

"Morning," said the ghost. "Say how do you do to my Auntie Edna."

"She can't come here," roared the children.

"Oh yes, she can," said the ghost. "She always comes here in August. Likes a bit of a change, does Auntie."

Auntie Edna was even worse, if possible. She sucked peppermint drops which smelled so strong that Mrs Brown kept asking the children what they were eating. She sang hymns in a high, squeaky voice. She followed the children all over the house. She said she loved kiddies, it was nice to be where there were two such nice kiddies.

Two days later the children came up to bed to find a third ghost in their room. "Meet Uncle Charlie," said the first ghost. The children groaned.

"And Jip," said the ghost. "Here, Jip, good dog, say hallo, then."

A large grey dog that you could see straight through came out from under the bed, wagging its tail. The cat gave a howl and ran away again. The children howled too, with rage, and got under the bedclothes.

The ghosts chatted to each other all night, and told long boring stories.

The children decided that something had to be done. They couldn't go on like this. "We must get them to go and live somewhere else," said Marian.

The problem was where. And how.

That Sunday they were going to see their uncle, who lived by himself in a big house. Plenty of room for ghosts. The children were very cunning. They asked the ghosts if they would like a drive in the country.

The ghosts said it might make a bit of a change.

On the way, the three ghosts and their dog sat on the back shelf of the car. Mr and Mrs Brown kept asking why there was such a strong smell of peppermint drops. They asked why the children were so restless, too. The fact was the ghosts kept shoving them.

The ghosts liked it at Uncle Dick's. They liked his colour television and they liked his fitted carpets. Nice and comfy, they said. "Why not settle down here?" said Simon, in an offhand sort of way.

"Couldn't do that," said the ghosts. "No children. Dull. We like a place with a bit of life to it."

All the way home in the car they ate toast. There were real toast-crumbs on the car floor and the children got the blame.

Then the children had a brilliant idea. At the end of their road there lived a Mr and Mrs Clark, who had a baby. No other children. Just one baby. And all day long the baby was bored. It sat in its pram in the garden and threw its toys out and cried.

"I wonder . . ." said Simon and Marian to each other.

They made friends with Mrs Clark. They did her shopping for her and took the baby for walks and washed her car.

Mrs Clark invited them to tea.

They said to the ghosts, "Would you like to go visiting again?" The ghosts said they wouldn't mind.

Mrs Clark gave the children ham sandwiches and chocolate cake. The ghosts watched the colour television. They said it was a nice big one, and they liked the big squashy sofa too. They went all round the house and said it wasn't at all a bad little place. Nice and warm, they said. Homely.

They *loved* the baby. "Ah!" said Auntie Edna. "There now . . . bless its little heart. Give us a smile, then, darling." They all sat round it and chattered at it and sang to it and told it stories.

And the baby loved the ghosts. It cooed and chuckled and smiled and it never cried all afternoon. Mrs Clark said she couldn't think what had come over it.

Well, I expect you can guess what happened. The ghosts moved down the road. Mrs Clark has the happiest baby in the world, Simon and Marian no longer have to share their bedroom with three other people, and the cat has come back.

Sir Ralph Richardson
I Had a Dog Once
Illustrated by
Sir Hugh Casson
KCVO

I had a dog once.

He was not exactly my own dog, he was more of a family dog; not of my choice as a pet. But I liked him.

He was a pug.

I liked him but he had some habits which I did not admire at all.

We had a garden, in Hampstead. Sometimes birds would visit us and settle on our lawn. If a bird was sitting there, this "pug"—"pug" for "pugnacious"?—would rush out and bark at the birds and frighten them away. Could not have been difficult for him to do as the dog was a great deal bigger than the birds but afterwards the dog would stroll about the lawn with an air of triumph that I did not much admire.

To oblige the family I would sometimes take the pug for walks. One day I took him with me when I went to paint a picture of sunlight on the waters of the Aldenham Reservoir at Elstree.

As I tried to paint, the dog rushed about a great deal, in and out of the bushes and along the water's edge.

After a while he came to me and looked up at me—these pugs have an eloquent look—and this look clearly said, "Come and see! There is trouble here!"

I got up from my painting and followed him.

There was trouble indeed.

A bird had been caught in the throat by the hook of a fisherman's cast. It could not fly, or indeed move at all, and was in a most unhappy state.

The pug looked me in the eye as if to say, "I think that we should do something about this."

I was able to set the bird free, and it flew away.

That pugnacious pug was, after all, a bit of a gent.

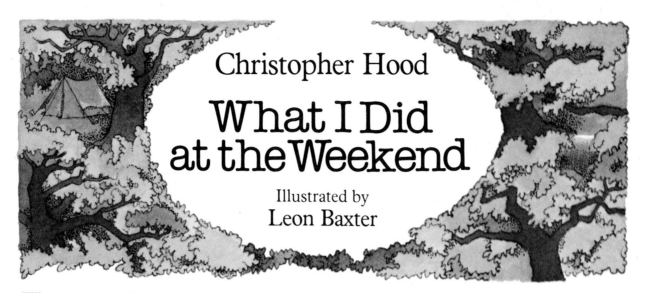

Christopher Hood

What I Did at the Weekend

Illustrated by
Leon Baxter

When we came home from school on Friday my father said we were going camping. This was exciting because the only camping my brother and I had done was sleeping in the tent in the back garden. My father said it was time we learned the ropes and we ought to realise the potential of the place we lived in instead of sitting about moping all the time. My brother wanted to know what a potential was and my father told him to shut up and find his sleeping bag. I suppose my father meant we ought to enjoy the mountains we live near; potential was a sort of word to make this sound important. He started pulling out the tent and the rucksack and the billycans and getting my mother to find things and changing his mind about what we ought to take.

So I sat and read my book until everything was ready and when it was we couldn't find my brother. Then my mother found him in the cupboard under the stairs and when my father asked what he thought he was doing he said he had been looking for the ropes to release the potential but when he couldn't find them he decided to sit and mope instead. My father told him to try and be sensible for two minutes and find his shoes and then we were ready. To get to the mountains we only had to cross a field and carefully cross a railway line and we were there; my mother stood at the door trying to get the baby to wave but he didn't understand and just looked at her and gurgled.

The mountains are covered by thick woods which are mostly fir trees but up the streams are some oak trees and some other ones my father doesn't know the name of. As soon as you start walking up a stream you're in another world where nobody can see you, full of dappled sunshine and waterfalls and pools. Some parts of the way are very steep and slippery and once I put down a bag of supplies and it rolled and bumped down nearly to the stream and my father said scrambled eggs for dinner and sent me to pick it up. When we got to the camping place which was a flat grassy bit among oak trees, we got busy putting up the tent and fetching firewood and water. The tent is only big enough for two so my father had brought along a sheet of polythene to make himself a shelter. He fixed it up to some trees using washing line and clothes pegs which kept popping off because the polythene was slippery. My brother wanted to know if that was the rope we were learning about and my father told him to shut up and get some more wood.

Some of the wood was rather damp and anyway my father isn't very good at fires; he has to use a lot of firelighters and strong language and lie on the ground blowing smoke in your eyes and bits of ash into the dinner. But camping dinners always taste nice in spite of the ash though the instant mashed potato didn't; as my father mixed it in it frothed up over the top of the billycan and went all over the fire, so some of it was burnt and some of it still dry and powdery. My father said he must have used the wrong ratio of water and my brother said whatever rate of water you used it still made the potato nasty, and my father told him to shut up and try and find some firewood which didn't feel like a wet sponge.

You need newly dead wood which is either lying on the ground or can be pulled down from the trees; you tie a small piece of wood to the end of a rope and throw it up so it winds round a dead bit of branch, then you pull it down with a sharp tug. My brother said *this* must be learning the ropes and my father told him to shut up and stand clear. Then when we were both well out of the way he pulled a branch down on his head. My brother said he didn't know much about the ropes himself and my father told him to shut up and find the sticking plaster but we'd forgotten to bring any. So my father tore a strip from the piece of old sheet we'd brought to use as a towel, and tied it round his head which wasn't bleeding much anyway. Then we built up the fire and made some tea and started feeling rather jolly, looking forward to the flamelight when it got dark.

I forgot to mention that we have a dog called Herbert who had come camping with us, and he suddenly started growling and barking fiercely and my father told him to shut up and the next thing that happened was that four firemen were standing round the fire carrying beaters and shaking their heads and going tut tut to each other. It seemed that somebody had seen the smoke and thought the forest was on fire, and even though it wasn't the Forestry Commission wouldn't have been very pleased and they had better things to do than keep coming up to somebody's camp fire, and my father looked very embarrassed and poured water on the fire and they went away again.

So we weren't feeling very jolly any more since we thought we'd have to go home because tea bags and eggs and sausages and soup and instant mashed potato aren't very nice when they're raw, but then my father had an idea and went off to see some friends of ours and borrow a camping stove. Our friends have a fierce dog called Mangler who is always starting fights so my father tied Herbert to a tree, and because it was beginning to get dark my brother and I went and sat in the tent and I got a torch out and read my book. At first Herbert was whining pitifully but after a while he stopped and when I looked out he'd chewed through the rope and disappeared. So I ran in the direction he had gone but I couldn't trace him so I sat in the tent and read my book again. Then I heard him barking and there was a crashing of bushes and a strange noise like horses' hooves only not so loud. My brother and I stepped out of the tent just as Herbert was driving about half a dozen sheep into the camp.

One of the sheep nearly ran into us because it had been running just past the tent but then it saw us and dodged and ran into the tent instead. Then it panicked and started jumping about and pulled all the tent pegs out and then the tent was running away and bleating and Herbert was chasing it and barking but I managed to get hold of him and told him he was naughty and my brother got excited and hit him with the loaf of French bread.

Luckily when the sheep ran through the undergrowth it left the tent behind so we went and picked it up. It was only torn slightly in two places but it was a nasty job trying to find the tent pegs; when my father had left the air had been lightly dusted with dark but now it was much thicker in the lightest places and under the trees it was nearly black. We were still busy trying to get the tent back up and looking around with torches when my father came back with the camping stove and used a lot of words which you aren't allowed to take to school. He said the sheep had no business on Forestry Commission land but where we live the sheep go everywhere including the back garden to eat the flowers if you leave the gate open. Anyway we found enough tent pegs to hold the tent up and my father made some tea and said goodnight and wrapped himself in his blankets and got into his shelter. We got into the tent and I read my book for a while but some of the pages were a bit difficult because of the hoof prints. We had a good night's sleep and I got up early in the morning. My father had a sheet of polythene as a groundsheet and his shelter was on slightly sloping ground so by now he had slid right out and lay covered in dew with Herbert snoozing contentedly on his head.

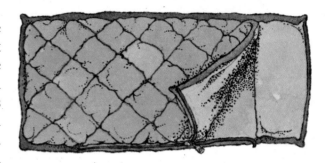

We had breakfast and found the missing tent pegs and tidied up the camp and then it was a fine and lovely day and we went exploring and played games. We played a sort of hide and seek with a lot of chasing and my brother got excited and lost his footing and fell down a short waterfall into a pool. So my father said hide and soak, ho ho, and we went back to camp and my brother hung up his clothes and dressed in a blanket and later on we played a game called Marauders where one of us guarded the camp and the other two crept up and attacked it. We had a very happy time and then had supper and cups of tea and sat up telling stories about Red Indians and Marauders and Pirates and then we went to bed. My father decided to sleep in the tent too which worked quite well and wasn't too squashed. My father got up in the middle of the night to go to the lavatory and when he came back my brother woke up and hit him with a shoe because he thought he was a Marauder.

In the morning my father looked out of the tent and said oh dear it looked like rain, and my brother got out of the tent and said it felt like rain too, and we quickly moved all the

supplies and the camping stove into the polythene shelter and cooked breakfast in there which worked quite well only the wet bread wasn't very nice. We put on our kagouls and went down to wash up in the stream, which was running deeper and faster because of the rain. We talked about what would happen if there was a big enormous flood and my brother got excited because he thought the school might be washed away; and my father told him to shut up and look what he was doing and then one of the billycans was floating away and my father had to jump in the stream to rescue it.

Then we went and sat in the shelter which had a sort of flat roof where a big puddle of water had gathered only we didn't realise that until the shelter collapsed and the puddle poured down my father's neck. He said it was time we went and we rushed around trying to pack things before they got soaked, and Herbert barked and my brother jumped up and down shouting: "Big enormous flood, big enormous flood", and my father told him to shut up and gave him a bundle to be careful with, but on the way down the bank my brother slipped and the bundle rolled into the stream and came open and we all had to rush about catching things as they floated away over waterfalls. I'd finished reading my book so I didn't mind about it very much. Everything else was soaking but we didn't lose anything important, just some cigarettes and one of my father's plimsolls which came off when he trod on a slippery rock and fell over and scrambled up again, and by the time he realised he wasn't wearing it it had gone. We looked for it all the way back down the stream but we couldn't see it. My father was hobbling and my brother thought perhaps he'd trodden on a poisoned thorn and would have to have his leg off and go about like Long John Silver. He asked my father if he'd buy a parrot if he had to have his leg off, and my father told him to shut up and come along and then we got home.

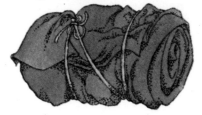

We all had baths and my brother had two because he got out of the first one no cleaner than when he got in. He said he'd been told to have a bath and no one had said anything about a wash. We went to bed early because it was school tomorrow and we were tired.

Next day at school the first lesson was Composition, so I opened my exercise book and copied down the title which was: "What I did at the Weekend". Then I got stuck because I couldn't think what to put.

Peter Cross

RUSH HOUR AT FITTLETHORPE HALT

Our headmaster,
Awful fat,
Wind blew off
Headmaster's hat.

Blew it under
A steam roller.
Headmaster chased
Blown off bowler.

Bowler bowled
Roller rolled
Imagine that!
Headmaster . . .

FLAT!

MARTIN
WADDELL
ILLUSTRATED BY
LEON BAXTER

Jean Kenward

Peculiar People

Illustrated by
Gillian Chapman

There was a Welshman
born in Wales
who munched a bag
of carpet nails,
a saw, a mallet
and a hammer—
and then he ate
a giant spanner!

The spanner, it
was big and wide.
When it was halfway
down inside
it stuck, and would
not budge a bit.

He was a MUG
to swallow it.

Down by the bus stop
alost and alone
I came upon old Mister
Bleary-and-Blown.
His trousers were twisted,
his scarf was awry,
his shirt tail was flapping—
he hadn't a tie—
his shoes were undone
and the laces were trailing . . .
and O what a whirling
and O what a wailing
the wind made about him
alost and alone,
till the bus came to get him—
old Bleary-and-Blown!

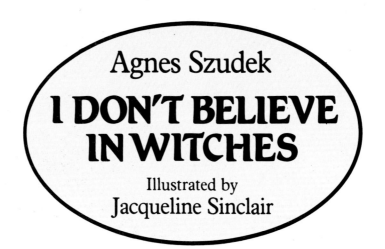

Agnes Szudek

I DON'T BELIEVE IN WITCHES

Illustrated by
Jacqueline Sinclair

It had been snowing for days, and a wild blizzard in the night had blown the snow into high, curving peaks. The countryside was white and still.

In the kitchen, Nonny finished off her porridge and said, "Mum, can I go and play in the snow?"

Nonny's mother said, "Yes, if you put on your cap and mittens. And remember, Nonny, don't go near Briony Hill."

"I won't," Nonny called as she closed the kitchen door.

Nonny's father was mending the old fence that had blown down during the night. "True enough," he said. "It's steep and dangerous. Keep away from Briony Hill."

"Yes, Dad," said Nonny.

Gramp was putting food on the bird-table. "Yip! It's swarming with witches, up Briony Hill. They'll snitch and snatch at you with their long nails. I know all about witches," he said. Gramp was old enough to know all about most things. But he couldn't make Nonny believe in witches.

"Oh, don't worry about me!" Nonny shouted back over her shoulder. "Witches? Huh!"

She played alone in the snow where she could still see the red chimney of her home. But when your world is covered with untouched snow, it's easy to move away without noticing.

Nonny rolled a snowball about until it was almost as big as herself. And when she was tired, she sat down to rest on a log. The branches of the trees behind her joined together overhead and made a tunnel that led uphill to a shady blue world. Nonny did not see the signpost deep in a snowdrift. Its half-hidden words said, BRIONY HILL.

She did not see the figure lying above on a twisted branch. She did not see one moist green eye watching her, nor the long crinkly ear trying hard to listen to her words.

The Oldest Witch in the World was resting among the briony, right over Nonny's head.

"Witches—huh!" Nonny was saying again and again. "Only grownups believe in witches." She showered the crispy snow about with her boots. Then she scooped some off the log and rubbed the frosted bark with her mitten. "I don't believe in witches. I never did, I still don't, and I never will!" she said, defiantly.

The old woman in the tree leaned over, trying hard to listen. Further and further she leaned until—Plooooff! She lost her balance and fell softly into the snow at Nonny's feet.

At first Nonny thought a giant crow had fallen from the sky, until the black bundle rose to its knees. The wrinkled face of the ancient witch looked up.

"What did you do that for, you little shrimp?" she snapped angrily.

"I-I-I- didn't do anything," began Nonny. "And, and, I don't believe in witches," she added, seeing the old woman's pointed hat and her black cloak lined with silver stars.

"Wha-a-a-at did you say?" screeched the witch, in a voice like a rusty saw. "You imp of mischief! You—you—don't you know who I am?"

"I don't know you at all," replied Nonny.

"*I* am Omeletta Haggis, the Oldest Witch in the World," said the witch, rising up to her full height. "Not a dribble of magic has escaped

my notice for three hundred years. And *you* have the sauce not to believe in witches!"

"No, I don't," said Nonny firmly, folding her arms.

The old woman leapt off the ground in a frenzy. Her cloak floated round her like an evening cloud. "Then you soon will, my little tadpole," she cried, and diving forward, she grabbed Nonny's arm and held her fast. At the same time, she swung her cloak around them both.

Nonny felt sharp nails digging into her arm. "They'll snitch and snatch at you with their long nails," Gramp had told her. But it was too late to think of that now. Nonny was pulled up into the shadowy blueness of Briony Hill. Silver stars shone in her eyes as though night had suddenly covered the earth.

On they walked up the hill, and when they neared the top, Nonny heard high-pitched shrieks and squeals in the distance. Omeletta Haggis threw back her cloak, and looking down on the other side of the hill, Nonny saw not one or two witches, but witches galore! They were **every**where, as far as she could see.

"Look you now, little miss, and say you don't believe in witches," said the old woman. And she tossed her head and laughed, "Heh! Heh! Heh!"

Nonny said nothing, but she looked. The witches were doing extraordinary things. They seemed to be practising skills on their broomsticks, the way she practised skills at P.E. in school. They were sitting on their broomsticks, whizzing down hill, showing their shiny buckled shoes and their long striped stockings. Some were using them like skateboards, doing daffy ducks, tick-tacking and pirouetting. They were having great fun.

"Oh yes, we need a holiday like everybody else," croaked Omeletta Haggis, seeing Nonny's astonished look. "It's not good to work without a break. But we're still witches, let me tell you. They're warming up for the big race of the day. Come and have a bite to eat before I start them off."

Nonny looked doubtfully at a cluster of stew-pots steaming over charcoal fires. Witch-cooks in purple aprons were stirring the pots with wooden ladles. Beside them were stalls with sausages strung up like half-moons and star-shaped toast to dip into red sorrel soup.

"Are they—are they really *all* witches?" whispered Nonny, as a bowl of soup and toast were thrust into her hands.

"Every magic one of them, and don't you forget it," said Omeletta Haggis. "It's time for the Witch of the Year Contest. They're waiting for me to start it."

"What do they have to do?" asked Nonny.

"Anything. It's a broomstick freestyle. The first one to reach that scarecrow yonder is Witch of the Year and gets a special badge."

"Oh, I love races. Could I join in?" Nonny asked eagerly, forgetting to be afraid.

"How can you? You haven't got a broomstick."

"I could borrow yours, if you're not using it." Nonny pointed to the broomstick under the witch's arm.

Omeletta Haggis smiled a wide empty smile, showing how many teeth she had lost. "The very thing," she said. "Off you go and see what you can do."

Nonny exchanged her soup bowl for the broomstick and got into line with all the witches who glowered at her and jostled her. She tried to arrange herself on her stomach on the bundle of twigs.

"Bold little thingummyjig, aren't you?" squawked the skinny witch next to Nonny. She put out a scrawny arm and felt Nonny's leg as though she didn't believe she was real.

Nonny drew her leg back and shuddered.

"Leave her be, Slimkin," crowed the witch on the other side. "Don't worry, she'll never win."

At that moment, Omeletta Haggis raised her wand. There was a sharp crack like a pistol shot and the race had started. Nonny pushed off with her legs and away she went, almost blinded by the black cloaks flapping about on either side of her. She hardly knew where she was going.

Snow shot up coldly into her face like sharp slaps. It was difficult to breathe with the icy wind cutting into her mouth. Down, down the hill went the race with howls and screams. Nonny was thinking she had never done anything so hard in her life when—WHAM! She collided with something solid that sent her spinning off the broomstick and up in the air. Then down she fell and landed astride the shoulders of the scarecrow winning-post.

Dozens of green eyes glared jealously up at Nonny. Waving arms tried to reach her and pull her down.

"She can't have won! She's a human child!"

"Disqualify her! She's not one of us!"

The noise was deafening as the witches began to shake the scarecrow from side to side.

"No, no! Leave me alone! Leave me alone!" shouted Nonny.

Just then Omeletta Haggis came hobbling down the hill. "Stop this frightful racket!" she commanded. "The race was fairly won by the little sprout on *my* broomstick. And don't dare to say it wasn't!"

She gathered Nonny up in her arms and placed her on the ground. "I hereby declare this little sprou—what's your name, child?"

"Nonny," said Nonny.

"I declare this little Nonny is Witch of the Year. Now do I hear clapping?"

Omeletta Haggis pinned a big round badge on Nonny's jacket, with the shape of a witch's hat on it. The other witches tried to look pleased and stretched their faces sideways in ugly smiles. They clapped their knotted fingers together and muttered under their breaths, as Omeletta Haggis flipped one leg over her broomstick and beckoned to Nonny.

Nonny climbed up and held on to the witch. It was like clasping a bag of bones, she thought. Then, like an arrow from a bow, the broomstick shot off into the sky over Briony Hill and away towards Nonny's house.

Minutes later, they landed neatly at the bottom of her garden, by a clump of fir trees. Snow sprayed up on either side.

"Oh, Miss Haggis! I do believe in witches, I do," gasped Nonny as she tumbled to the ground. "I'll believe in witches for ever and ever."

"I should think so too," said the Oldest Witch in the World, hovering above her. "And we're not all bad, you know. There's good and bad everywhere. Until we meet again, my little newt! Magicoo-switchback!" she shrieked, and turning a somersault in the air, she zoomed away—upside down.

Nonny's father and Gramp had finished their work and were warming their toes in the kitchen as she went in. At once Gramp spotted the badge. "Bet you got that from a witch," he said, with a little smile.

Nonny smiled back and nodded. Of course Gramp would know. He was old enough to know all about most things.

One day Basher the Alley Cat finds
a sack of coal lying in the street.

A sudden shower of rain sends him
dashing into the museum for shelter.

As soon as the rain stops
he leaves, carrying the sack.

Basher is not very interested in museums.
He has no respect for old things.

At once a voice shouts "Thief"!
The alarm is raised

and everyone chases Basher. Meanwhile
a real thief opens the mummy's case.

He grabs the priceless
Egyptian mummy,

drops it into his bag
and slinks out.

In a panic Basher tries
to fling the sack away

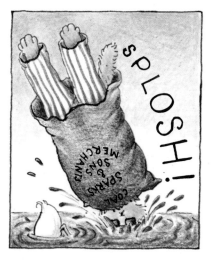

but trips

and falls head first

into a muddy pond.

He is stuck in the sack and black with coal dust.

Seeing the strange black figure hobbling along the crowd scatters with screams of terror.

Basher's friends the Alley Cats do not believe in ghosts,

but at the sight of Basher

Klaws, the leader of the gang, faints with fright.

At that moment a thunderstorm breaks overhead.

As the rain washes off   the mud and the coal dust   the Alley Cats recognise their old friend Basher.

Just then Police Dog Barker goes by. He has arrested Snatcher Slickpaws, a top international sneak thief. Basher decides crime doesn't pay after all.

Philip Ennis

The New Aerodrome

Illustrated by
John Thompson-
Steinkrauss

I have seen the heron stand
Where hangars now are standing,
And rabbits burrow in the ground
Where aeroplanes are landing;
I have seen, oh! I have seen—
It fills my heart with grieving—
The warblers knit their nests in corn
With skill of woman's weaving.
But now the concrete and the roar
And days that were are mine no more.

I have heard the vixen whine
Where engines now are whining,
And plovers call along the night
Where runway arcs are shining;
I have heard, so often heard—
The memory fills with yearning—
The chorusing of flocks of birds
As dark to day is turning,
But now, with sodium vapour bright
The day is day, and so is night.

I have felt the weasel's scan
Where radar now is scanning,
And dragonflies invade the place
The jet-streamed air is fanning.
I have felt, so strangely felt—
It makes the memory quiver—
A living silence, calm and soft
As mist upon a river;
But now the engine rules the day
And all the life has slipped away.

Colin
Hawkins

It's a Fact

snap!

Heaviest Spider:
A female tarantula of the
long-haired species
collected in Brazil in 1945.
It measured 9½ in. across
the leg and weighed
almost 3oz.

104

Oldest parrot: Jimmy, a red and
green Amazon parrot, owned by
Mrs Bella Ludford of Liverpool
hatched in captivity in 1870
and lived 104 years in his
original brass cage.

Heaviest baby:
According to the New York Medical Record of 1879, Mrs Anna Bates produced a baby weighing $23\frac{1}{2}$ lbs. The mother was 7ft $5\frac{1}{2}$ in. and was married to a giant, making them the tallest married couple on record.

Oldest bride and bridegroom: Dyura Avramovich, reportedly aged 101, married Yula Zhivich, admitting to 95, in Belgrade, Yugoslavia in 1973.

Just Married

Person most often struck by lightning:
Roy Sullivan, the human lightning conductor of
Virginia, USA, 7 times, in the course of which
he has lost eyebrows, hair and a toenail
and been in hospital
for burns.

Heaviest cat:
Tiger, a nine-year-old
long-haired, part-persian
who scales a constant
42-43 lbs.

Oddest meal:
M. "Mangetout" Lotito ate a complete bicycle, including tyres, over a period of 15 days in Every, France, in 1977.

Inspired by the Guinness Book of Records.

Heaviest chicken:
Weirdo, a rooster of the White Sully breed developed in California, reportedly weighed 22 lbs., killed two cats and crippled a dog.

Weirdo

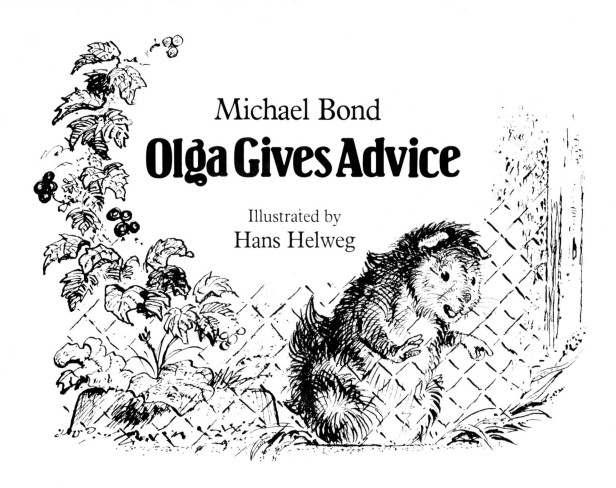

Michael Bond
Olga Gives Advice

Illustrated by
Hans Helweg

Graham was in love. There was no doubt about it. Olga first noticed it one morning when he came round the side of the house, crawled slowly past her hutch as if it didn't even exist, and then walked with unseeing eyes 'slap-bang into the closed door of Mr Sawdust's shed.

If it had been anyone else—Noel, the cat, or even Fangio, the hedgehog—they would have made a quick recovery and gone on their way. But in Graham's case, being a slow-mover at the best of times, it took him some while to sort himself out. Having been knocked off course he moved on in the wrong direction and wasn't seen again until after lunch.

Having partaken of several succulent blades of grass, carefully folded in two and eaten from the middle so that she would get the most benefit from the least possible effort, Olga was about to retire to her bedroom for an afternoon nap when she heard a rustle in the nearby shrubbery.

This time she was better prepared. "Watch out!" she squeaked, as Graham drew near. "Wheeeeee! Wheeeeeeeeeee!"

Graham paused and gazed up at her with a vacant expression on his face.

"Aren't you going to have your bread and milk?" asked Olga. "Mrs Sawdust put some out for you specially."

"Food!" Graham scoffed at the idea. "That's all you guinea-pigs ever think about. There *are* other things in life, you know."

Olga drew herself up. "There won't be if you carry on like that," she said. "You won't *have* a life if you carry on like that. You'll be all shell and bones."

Graham considered the matter for a moment. "You're quite right," he said. "Quite right. I *must* keep up my strength." And without further ado he moved towards the bowl which was standing outside the kitchen door.

Olga preened herself as a sound of steady lapping filled the air. She gave a sigh. There was no doubt about it. Guinea-pigs *knew* about things. It was something they were born with. How the other animals had managed before she came on the scene goodness only knew. There was simply no one else to turn to for advice.

She waited for a while and then, during a pause in the lapping, posed the question which was uppermost in her mind.

"What's she like?"

Graham didn't answer for a moment or two. The fact of the matter was, although he wouldn't have admitted it to Olga, hunger had got the better of him and he had a large piece of bread stuck in his throat. Turning his head away he pretended he was thinking hard. Olga, who thought he was choking with emotion, waited patiently.

"She's big," admitted Graham at last, "and... er ... well, I suppose you'd just say ... she's big. Big for her size, that is ..."

Olga, her feminine instincts aroused, squeaked impatiently. "There must be something else about her," she exclaimed. "How about her eyes?"

"They're big too," said Graham. "She's big all over."

Olga took a deep breath. "I mean ... what colour are they?"

Graham busied himself with the bread and milk again. Being in love made you hungry. "I don't know," he said at last.

"You don't know! *You don't know!*" Olga could hardly believe her ears. Tortoises! No wonder they had a reputation for being slow.

"You *must* have seen them," she said.

For some reason or other Graham seemed to find the question slightly embarrassing. "Well," he said between mouthfuls. "Yes, and then again . . . no. I mean, I know they're there. They must be. But the thing is, well, she's big, you see, and they're a bit high off the ground."

Olga gazed at Graham as he stood there looking at her helplessly, a dribble of milk running down his chin. She didn't like to say anything, but she couldn't help feeling that if she'd been his new friend she might not have wanted to look at him either.

"There must be something else about her," she exclaimed impatiently. "What does she talk about? What does she say?"

"Well, er . . ." Graham shifted uneasily under Olga's piercing stare. "She hasn't actually said anything . . . yet.

"But I know she'd like to," he added hastily. "It's just that she's very quietly spoken, and being so big her voice is a long way off the ground."

Olga digested this latest piece of information. Happy though she was in her house with all its "mod. cons." as Karen Sawdust called them, there were times when she wished she could get out into the world and see things for herself. Apart from that, Graham's continual harping on the size of his new friend was beginning to irritate her.

"I once knew a giant guinea-pig," she began, her imagination getting the better of her. "The largest guinea-pig ever known in the whole world. He was so big I always knew when he was coming to see me because it got dark early. And he had wonderful fur. I mean . . . all guinea-pigs' fur is nice compared to other animals, like cats, for instance, but . . ."

Olga broke off. Graham had disappeared. Completely and utterly disappeared.

"Wheeeeeee!" she squeaked in disgust. And she went into her bedroom in a fit of pique. If people wanted her advice about matters the least they could do was stay and listen. Apart from that, she'd been rather enjoying building up her story and she spent most of that afternoon busy with her daydream, storing it up in her memory so that she could bring it out later when she had a better audience.

But gradually, as the day wore on, her thoughts returned more and more to Graham. He'd looked so forlorn as he'd blinked shortsightedly up at her. Something would have to be done about the matter.

Olga reached a decision. She went into her dining-room and gave voice to a loud squeak. The kind of squeak which she reserved for

moments of great importance. Moments when she wanted to summon an audience.

"Graham's in love?" repeated Fangio, the hedgehog. "What does that mean?"

Olga sighed. "It's something you wouldn't know about on account of your prickles," she said stiffly, "but it can be very painful."

She hesitated, wondering whether to try out her new story, but thought better of it as Noel, the cat, came into view.

"What's up now?" he asked sleepily.

Olga told him about her earlier conversation with Graham, embroidering it a little here and there in order to make it as interesting as possible.

"If it's as big as all that," said Noel hastily, "*I'm* certainly not going down the garden to look for it. It's bad enough having Karen Sawdust and her friends playing war games without being trampled by a giant."

For once Olga rather regretted her vivid imagination.

"Well, perhaps it's not as big as all that," she admitted grudgingly. But Fangio and Noel had gone.

And then it happened. There was a pounding of feet and suddenly, without warning, a large, round shape loomed up in front of her. Olga gave a shriek of terror and scuttled into her bedroom as fast as her legs would carry her.

"There! I told you to be careful." Karen's voice reached Olga through the hay. "Now you've frightened her. I expect she wondered what on earth it was."

"It's only a tin hat," said her friend defensively.

"It may only be a tin hat to you," said Karen Sawdust severely, "but to a guinea-pig it must look like a giant."

There was another patter of feet, this time in the opposite direction, and then silence.

Olga stirred as the words sank in. "Tin hat ... giant ..."

Suddenly she put two and two together. "Tin hat ... giant ..." Graham had been in love with a tin hat all the time! No wonder he hadn't got anywhere. She couldn't wait to tell the others ...

And then she paused, her romantic side taking over. Better to have loved a tin hat and lost than never to have loved at all.

Already an ending to her story was taking shape. That's what she would do. She would tell Graham a story that would be so good, so exciting, it would take his mind off the problem.

"Wheeee!" Olga gave a sigh of contentment as she snuggled down in her hay again. "And it'll be so much better for him in the long run!"

Richard Hales
Animal Tonguetwisters
Illustrated by
Margaret Chamberlain

Don't alarm a llama in pyjamas

Don't greet a cheetah on the street

Don't do a samba with a mamba

Don't goad a goat into deceit

Don't crack a croc with a crowbar

Don't strike a stoat with a stick

Don't cosh a cuckoo with a caber

Don't bash a budgie with a brick.

Don't abscond on a Honda with an anaconda

Don't bake a snake inside a cake

Don't assume a puma's wearing bloomers

Don't grill a gorilla while awake

Don't tease a weasel with the measles

Don't fool a flea that's got the flu

Don't entice a bison that's got flies on

Don't get a gnu into a stew.

The Boxer

I am a merry boxer
I get into the ring
Wallop! Wallop Thud! I go
Until the bell goes ding!

When the bell goes ding! again
I go back to my stool
And stare at my opponent
The ~~silly~~ ugly little fool!

Ding there goes the bell again
I rush back to the bout.
Wallop! Wallop Blat-Thud-OWW!
Nine - ten - OUT!

Signed by Spike Milligan

John Yeoman

Nature Notes

Pictures by
Quentin Blake

Butterfly nets and jars and baskets,
Out to the woods and fields we troop—
Members of the Maypole Common
Local Natural History Group.

Scrambling through the prickly gorses,
Wading in mud up to our knees,
Chasing butterflies, hunting beetles,
Finding foxholes, climbing trees.

Tim Pitt-Withins finds a mole-hill
(Desperate to catch a mole, is Tim),
Gives it a prod to see what happens;
Doesn't get the mole but the mole gets him.

Studying catkins, Mr Gamble
Closely examines an unusual bunch.
In the meantime, forty-seven
Hungry birds have finished his lunch.

Colonel Tinder stands in a clearing,
Polishing his monocle gleaming bright,
Hoping to glimpse a woodland creature, and
Very annoyed that there's none in sight.

Little Miss Whysper, dressed in muslin,
Sights some caterpillars, makes a dash,
Pops them into her handy jamjar;
Then breaks out in a nasty rash.

Miss Magee, who's fond of pondlife,
Trusts her weight on some floating logs,
Empties her wellies and finds eight tadpoles,
Two fat toads and nineteen frogs.

Lady Marchbanks, quite exhausted,
Sits on a stone for a little rest.
While she's dozing two smart jackdaws
Unpick her hat to build a nest.

Reverend Powler, mad on fungi,
Gathering kinds that have never been seen;
Tasting a few to prove they're edible,
Rolling his eyes and turning green.

Stings and bites and bumps and scratches,
Back from the woods and fields we troop—
Members of the Maypole Common
Local Natural History Group.

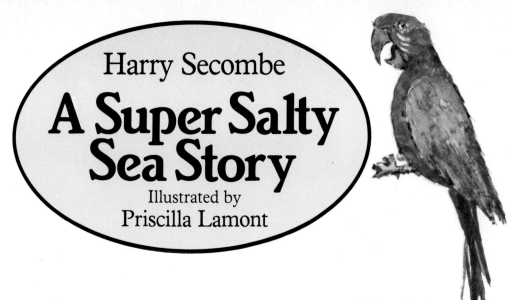

A Super Salty Sea Story

Harry Secombe

Illustrated by
Priscilla Lamont

The ship lay becalmed on a glassy sea and the sails hung lifelessly from the masts. Below decks the crew sat sweating in their bunks. They were very bored.

"I spy with my little eye something beginning with 'P'," said the Mate.

"Parrot," said Polly, the ship's parrot, who was perched on the cook's shoulder.

"Shut up you stupid bird." The Mate hated parrots, especially ones that could spell.

"Don't you call my parrot stupid," cried the Cook, heaving a belaying pin at the Mate.

"Yah! Missed me." The Mate stuck out his tongue.

"We are all getting very childish," remarked Cecil Keaton, a deckhand and amateur photographer. He was busy cleaning his camera. For days he had been trying to get a photograph of the whole crew on deck, but the skies had been too grey. He looked out of the porthole. It was still too cloudy.

There was silence for a few minutes as the dozen members of the crew sat or lay on their bunks and thought about various things. Tom Appleyard, the Bosun, thought about his wife and eight quarrelsome children who would be waiting for him at the quayside when they docked—if they docked. Arthur Holroyd, Ship's Carpenter, flicked a bead of sweat from the end of his nose and thought about steak and kidney pudding. He *always* thought about steak and kidney pudding. Jack Priam, deck hand, his eyes crossed with concentration, attempted to darn yet another hole in his sock, wishing all the while that he was back home in Portsmouth.

"I spy with my little eye something beginning with 'B'," said Polly the parrot, suddenly breaking the silence.

"Belaying pin!" shouted the Mate, seizing the object that the Cook had hurled at him and throwing it at the parrot. It struck the Cook on the head, and in no time he and the Mate were struggling on the floor between the bunks.

"Hit him. Hit him," cried Polly, fluttering around the cabin.

In less time than it takes to tell, all the crew were fighting with each other—it was something to do to relieve the boredom.

"What's all this, then?" The Captain stood in the doorway, his hands on his hips. He had been awakened from a lovely sleep by the noise and was very angry.

"It was the Mate," shrilled the parrot.

"That bird's a liar," shouted the Mate.

"Now, now. Calm down." The Captain hated fights. He was sixteen stone and was too fat to run away. He tried to think of some way of soothing his crew. They had been a long time at sea and had not had a decent meal for ages. No wonder they were fractious. He looked out of the porthole and saw, to his surprise, that the sun was coming out.

"Mind my camera," yelled Cecil Keaton, trying to shield his precious instrument from the fighting sailors.

The Captain had a sudden idea. "The sun's out, lads. Come on Keaton, now's your chance to take that picture of all of us. It'll be a lovely souvenir of the voyage."

With much grumbling the crew disentangled themselves and scrambled up on deck. Indeed the sun was shining at last, and there was a slight creaking in the rigging.

"Hurry up and get your picture," said the Captain, eyeing the sails, "there's a wind coming up."

Cecil Keaton set up his camera with his back to the ship's rail and made all the crew line up alongside the stern. They jostled each other

for the best position and only the Captain's presence stopped them from fighting again. Polly kept repeating the photographer's instructions until that normally gentle person threatened to wring its neck. He crouched underneath the black cloth covering the back of the camera and had difficulty getting all the crew in the picture, which to him, in the viewfinder, was upside down.

"Back a bit," he called from under his cloth, and the crew moved back a bit.

"A bit more please." They moved back further to the edge of the ship's stern. "I think that's about it," he started to say, when Polly yelled "Back a bit!", and all the crew fell overboard into the sea, Captain, parrot and all.

Now Cecil, suddenly unable to see anything at all, decided that he had better move back himself. "Stay there," he cried, grabbing at the legs of his tripod. Unfortunately he lost his balance and over he went with his camera.

Just then a breeze sprang up. The sails filled out, and the ship put on speed, leaving the crew struggling in its wake. The last thing they saw before they went down was the name of their ship painted in big white letters on the stern ... "MARIE CELESTE".

Mousework
Michelle Cartlidge

Mouse Waiter

Mouse Secretary

Mouse Hairdresser

Mouse Gardener

Mouse Balloon Seller

Mouse Ballet Dancer

Mouse Dressmaker

More Mousework on Page 72

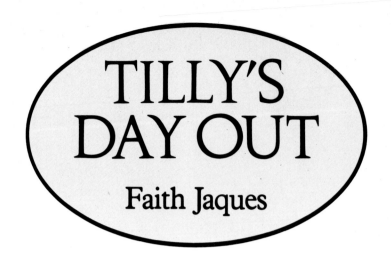

TILLY'S DAY OUT

Faith Jaques

One glorious summer's day Tilly the little wooden doll was watering the flowers when her friend Edward came to call.

"I've got a wonderful idea," said Edward. "Let's have a day out!"

"A day out?" said Tilly with surprise. "Where? Doing what?"

"We could slip through the fence into the garden next door," said Edward. "There's a sandpit there, and a paddling pool. Don't you think it would be fun?"

"Not much," said Tilly bluntly. "But if you want to go, I'd better go with you." She packed her shawl and Edward's scarf in her bag, took down the umbrella, and they set off.

They trudged through the long grass until at last they reached the garden fence. Edward helped her through.

He led Tilly across a lawn to a big square of sand set into the grass. Beyond it was a huge round plastic object. "That's the paddling pool," Edward said. "We might have a swim later."

"Swim!" shrieked Tilly in horror. "Get wet all over? Not me!"

"Well, let's lie in the sun for a while," said Edward patiently and helped her into the sandpit. Then he lay down with a sigh of contentment. Tilly sat primly beside him.

It was very hot. "My varnish will melt," complained Tilly.

Edward opened the umbrella and stuck it in the sand. "Sit under that," he suggested. "I'm going to have a snooze."

Tilly arranged herself in the shade of the umbrella. A wasp hovered around them, and an ant wandered over her apron.

"Oh do go away!" she said irritably, flicking her shawl at it. It seemed hours until Edward woke up. He saw a bucket and spade lying on the sand and picked them up. "I'll make a sandcastle," he said brightly. He made a mound of sand with his paws and put a row of sandpies on top. Tilly watched scornfully.

"Is that meant to be a castle?" she enquired.

Edward looked sadly at the messy pile of sand. "Perhaps it is a bit lopsided," he admitted.

The sun beat down on them and Tilly felt sticky and bored. "Isn't there anything else to do?" she asked.

There was a plastic boat half-buried in the sand. Edward hauled it out and cried, "Of course! We'll go for a sail!"

Edward dragged the boat over to the paddling pool and stood on tiptoe to look over the side. "It's lovely!" he called to Tilly. "Come on!"

Tilly gathered up her things and stumped towards him. A large rubber ball lay on the grass and Edward pushed it to the pool and heaved it over to the edge; it landed in the water with a satisfying splash. He sat on the side and tipped the boat into the water, and then helped Tilly climb up. She sat beside him as he hooked the boat with the umbrella and held it steady. Holding his paw, she nervously dropped into the boat.

Tilly sat in the bows and Edward lodged himself behind the funnel, fixing up the umbrella and her shawl to make a sail. Then he pushed off, and the little boat moved smoothly out towards the centre of the pool.

Tilly cheered up at once. The waves lapped gently round the boat as it glided swiftly along, and the sail fluttered gaily in a strong breeze.

"This is fun!" cried Tilly. "It's quite an adventure!"

The boat sailed on until they were quite near to the floating rubber ball. Tilly began to realise that the water was getting choppy, and the boat was rocking from side to side.

"Edward!" she cried in alarm. "It's not safe! The wind's got into the sail and we'll blow over!"

At that moment a powerful gust caught the sail and the boat keeled over so far that the funnel dipped into the water. It righted itself but water had poured down the funnel and inside the boat. It started to sink lower and lower in the water.

"Oh Tilly!" howled Edward. "We're sinking! What shall we do!"

They were close to the floating ball. "Quick, Edward!" cried Tilly. "Grab the umbrella and jump on to the ball!"

Edward was so frightened he obeyed her instantly. He made a desperate leap at the ball and landed, sprawled on top of it.

Tilly was thrown into the water as the boat capsized. "The umbrella!" she screamed to Edward. "Hold it out!"

He thrust it down to her and Tilly hung on like grim death as he pulled her up the side of the ball.

Tilly struggled up to the top and clung to Edward's fur as he used the umbrella to steer towards the edge of the pool. The ball swayed back and forth in the restless waves until at last they reached calm water.

Edward clambered on to the rim and pulled Tilly up after him. She was wet, tired, and extremely cross. He helped her to the ground and she started to squeeze the water out of her dress.

"Edward," she said grimly, "if this is your idea of a day out, all I can say is I'd just as soon stay at home. Better safe than sorry, that's what *I* say!"

Edward apologised. "It was an accident," he said humbly.

"It certainly was!" sniffed Tilly. "But least said, soonest mended. Now let's get home quick!"

Edward took the umbrella and the bag. "I'll lead the way. Are you quite sure you can manage?" he asked solicitously.

"Of course!" retorted Tilly. "I'm not damaged, only wet!"

So they set out on the homeward journey.

Damp and bedraggled, they eventually reached the fence and scrambled through it. They trekked through the long grass on the other side until at last they were home again in Tilly's cosy little house. They were exhausted.

Tilly dried herself thoroughly and hung up her shawl to dry. Then she lit a candle-stub and made Edward put his feet near it to dry them. Soon they began to feel much better.

"Well," said Edward, stretching out in his chair, "as I've said before, there is *nothing* so useful as a good strong umbrella!"

"How right you are," agreed Tilly. "It's saved us from disaster. But all's well that ends well!"

She settled herself comfortably, and took out her sewing. "I'll get on with this," she said, "and perhaps you'd like to have forty winks."

There was no reply from Edward. He was already fast asleep.

Mouse Window Cleaner

Mouse Doctor

Mouse Photographer

Mouse Musician

Mouse Carpenter

Mouse Roadsweeper

Mouse Librarian

Doormouse

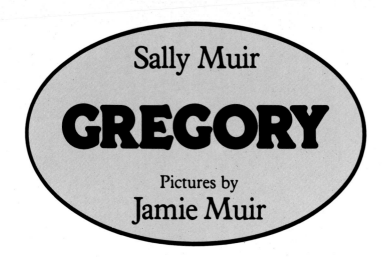

Sally Muir

GREGORY

Pictures by
Jamie Muir

Gregory was an exceptionally stupid rabbit. His brain was so small that you could hear it rattling around inside his head as he hopped. He was also a little shortsighted, which did not help.

So when he hopped up to a concrete mushroom in his next-door neighbour's garden and took a huge bite out of it no one was at all surprised. Then when his two front teeth fell out everyone just laughed and said unkindly, "How typical!"

Gregory took this remark to heart. Sadly he picked up his teeth and popped them into a foxglove which he hung round his neck. "I'll show 'em," he muttered through his gums, and hopped off to seek his fortune . . . and two new teeth.

He decided to go to London—to Harley Street—to get them fixed by a Brilliant Dentist. But being shortsighted he misread the signpost and set off in the wrong direction. He had gone a long way—towards Lincoln, not London—when he saw an extremely sleek, handsome rabbit sitting on a tuffet smiling and showing off his pure white teeth.

"This is the Great Carrot-Eating Competition," the sleek, handsome rabbit announced. "I invite anyone to try and beat my record." And he smiled a smug smile.

"Please, mister, where did you get your teeth?" asked Gregory politely.

The smug rabbit pretended that he had not seen him. "Do I hear a voice?"

"Down here," said Gregory.

"Ah yes. Well, young rabbit, do you want to challenge me to a carrot-eating comp ... " There he stopped and pushed his nose up against Gregory's face.

"You have no teeth at all! You are a toothless rabbit!" He laughed unkindly. "In which case I challenge you to a carrot-*sucking* competition!" And he laughed immoderately.

Gregory turned, muttered "I'll show 'em" through his gums, and hopped off.

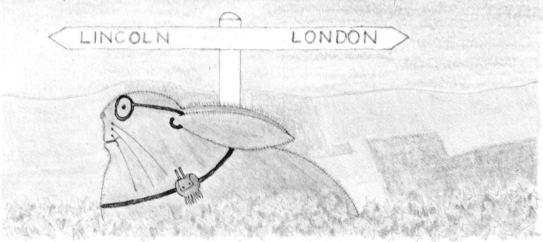

A mile or so on Gregory saw an orange lying by the side of the road. It reminded him that he had once seen a man being comical at a picnic by wearing false teeth cut from the peel of an orange. He picked it up, peeled it, cut the peel into teeth shapes and carefully fitted it where his own teeth had been. Although he had not got a mirror he felt that they probably looked rather good.

But two squirrels eating nuts underneath a hazelnut tree gave him one look and tore off into the woods, squeaking: "A monster! A monster! A terrible, terrible monster!"

Sadly, Gregory took out his beautiful new orange-peel teeth. He did not want to frighten anybody.

While he was burying them, he met some worms.

"I've lost my teeth," he told them. "Any ideas where I could borrow a pair until I get my own glued back?"

"No use asking us. We've never had teeth, and we've never missed them," said the worms, in the gloomiest way. But when they wormed up closer and had a good look at Gregory they began to laugh.

"A very funny sight! A very funny sight indeed!" said the worms, and thanked him kindly for making them laugh as they had not had a good laugh for a long, long time.

"It was nothing," said Gregory through clenched gums. And on he hopped.

Around midday he saw an aged cow chewing a mouthful of daisies and grass, and staring at nothing with half-closed eyes.

"Excuse me, madam," said Gregory. "Could you advise me as to my teeth?"

The cow continued chewing. Slowly she turned her head until she was looking straight at him. A huge smile crept across her face, from horn to horn, and she let out a great bellow of delight:

"You've no teeth! Did you know that? Did you know that you lack front teeth?" She wrenched a fresh mouthful of grass from between Gregory's feet and lumbered away, chortling: "No teeth at all! No teeth at all! That dim-looking rabbit's got no teeth at all!"

Gregory, nearly in tears, sat down and sucked his ear.

"Good for nothing, that's what I seem to be," he sighed. "My lack of teeth a laughing matter for old cows and gloomy worms. What I'll have to do is . . . I'll have to end it all."

Gregory strode into the middle of the road and lay down across it, theatrically.

But it was a very minor road and Gregory got bored waiting to be run over and fell asleep.

He woke up in the middle of the afternoon to find a boy with a bicycle standing over him.

"Hello," said the boy.

Gregory smiled foolishly. Then, remembering that he was toothless, he put a paw over his mouth.

"Don't worry, I haven't got any teeth either!" said the boy, pointing to the gap where his two front teeth should have been.

"Oh, how wonderful!" said Gregory. "Are you going to London, too? To have yours put back by the Brilliant Dentist in Harley Street?"

"No, but neither are you. This is the road to Lincoln," said the boy, but not unkindly. "Why don't you climb into my basket? I am on my way to London to sell my white mice Gladys and Cecil because I am too poor to keep them in the manner to which they are accustomed. My name is Daniel."

Gladys and Cecil turned out to be artistes and would not speak to Gregory. Instead they practised their *entrechats* in a corner of the basket, frowning at Daniel when he went over a bump in the road and jogged them off balance.

London was quite a big place but the Brilliant Dentist was not hard to find. On a shiny brass plate on the first house they came to was written:
Number One Harley Street
Brilliant Dentist

They all went in together. To pass the time while they were waiting for the Brilliant Dentist to see Gregory, Gladys and Cecil did a graceful *pas de deux* on a table in the middle of the room. Daniel explained to Gregory that he had begun by training Gladys and Cecil in simple tricks but they had recently become more ambitious and had taken up the ballet.

When a little bell rang, Daniel took Gregory upstairs and put him in the special chair. The Brilliant Dentist, who was very tall and wore a white coat, listened carefully to Gregory's story and nodded. In a few moments he had glued Gregory's teeth back into position. Then he

cleaned them with a brush and gave Gregory a tube of toothpaste and the brush to keep them shiny.

Gregory was ecstatic. Silently he clasped the Dentist's hand—as best he could. Daniel too, was happy, but a little worried as he had no

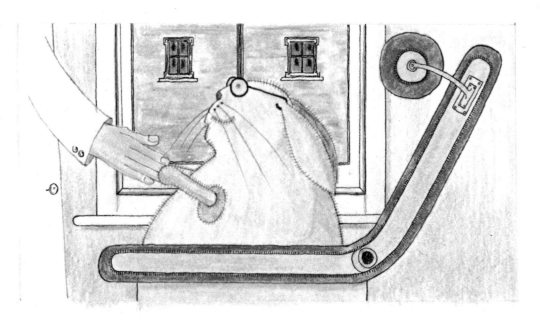

money to pay the Dentist his fee.

The problem was cleverly solved by Gladys and Cecil. They had been performing *The Sacrificial Dance of the Chosen One* from a Russian ballet called *Rite of Spring* in the hope of being discovered. The Dentist, who was not only Brilliant but also Keen on Art, watched and at the end clapped and cheered and was obviously so impressed that Daniel gave

Gladys and Cecil to the Dentist in lieu of payment.

Gladys and Cecil were too preoccupied with bowing and curtseying and wondering what to perform for their encore to notice that they had changed hands.

Gregory and Daniel arrived home just in time for Gregory to enter the Great Carrot-Eating Competition, and to beat the smug, sleek rabbit with the pure white teeth. This won Gregory great glory ... and four tons of carrots.

Later that evening, as he and Daniel lay on the grass after a huge supper of carrot stew, carrot juice, and carrot jelly, Gregory gave his new teeth one last brush and said happily:

"I showed them!"

Cynthia Mitchell
Sally Slater's Alligator

Picture by
Frances Livens

This tale began when Sally Slater
Bought a baby alligator,
Showed it to her friends at school
Then left it in her garden pool,
And, being more careless than she ought,
Gave it not another thought.
The alligator had no wish
To starve to death; it ate the fish,
It ate the tadpoles and the frogs
And several passing cats and dogs.
Then, roaming far and wide by night
To sate its growing appetite,
It ate a fox, a bearded goat,
A pony with a shaggy coat,
A brindled cow, a full-grown stag,
An early postman and his bag.
The missing mail caused quite a stir
And Sally's friends then said to her,
"What happened to your alligator?"
"It died, poor thing," lied Sally Slater.
Obligingly an hour later
Sally's alligator ate her
And dropping dead of indigestion
Proved her truthful on this question.

Eunice McMullen

JUST IMAGINE

Illustrated by
Nigel McMullen

Jane had too much imagination for her own good. And the day came
when it got her into real trouble . . .

It started at breakfast. Jane's father was so busy reading his paper that he was not paying attention to his scrambled eggs. Jane watched them slithering down his shirtfront and on to the table.

"He eats just like a pig!" she thought with disgust.

That was the first time it happened. Suddenly, in place of her father, Jane saw a pig sitting at the table! She was so startled that she jumped up, knocking her own plate to the floor.

"For goodness sake, Jane! Why don't you look what you're doing?" snapped her mother. "You spend far too much time daydreaming. Anybody who didn't know you would think you had the manners of a pig!"

"But it wasn't ..." started Jane, pointing across the table. She stopped as she met her father's eyes peering over the top of his newspaper. "You wouldn't understand," she sighed.

"Probably not," said her mother. "Now go and change that skirt before you're late for school. You've spilt egg all over it."

At school, it happened again. Jane was sitting quietly in room eight gazing out of the window. It was a maths lesson with Miss Prigg, so, of course, she wasn't paying attention.

"You, child, stop daydreaming!" said Miss Prigg, who could never remember anyone's name. "Oh, it's you again! What's your name?"

"Jane Adams, Miss Prigg," said Jane politely.

"Well, Jane Adams, I've warned you before about daydreaming. One of these days it's going to get you into serious trouble."

"Old witch!" thought Jane. Then she jumped to her feet in horror.

Miss Prigg was sailing round the room on a broomstick, chanting the seven times table. The class was in uproar. All the children were out of their seats, trying to dodge Miss Prigg as she zoomed over their heads. A moment later everything had returned to normal—well, almost. Miss Prigg and the children were back in their places, and Jane was on the floor with the contents of her desk scattered around her.

"Jane Adams! What have you been doing?" screeched Miss Prigg. "Pick those things up immediately. Now, children, we'll continue with the seven times table."

The room hushed and Jane, who was relieved to have got away with it so lightly, slid behind her desk and hoped that nobody would say anything to her for the rest of the lesson. As soon as the bell rang, she rushed into the playground, away from Miss Prigg's inquisitive gaze. She wanted to be by herself to think, but she was out of luck. She ran smack-bang into Billy Briggs, the school bully. He really was a revolting boy! Jane couldn't remember ever seeing him without a runny nose and he never used a handkerchief to wipe it.

"What have you been up to, Adams?" asked Billy, leering forward and pinching Jane hard on the arm.

"None of your business, Briggs!" said Jane bravely. Then she thought, "I wonder?" and said aloud, "You watch yourself, Briggs, or I'll turn you into a . . ."

Even before she had finished saying it, Billy Briggs was the fattest, hairiest spider she had ever seen. Jane grinned with delight as she saw him trying to scuttle away. "Should I step on him? No!" she decided. She had a much better idea. She picked up the wriggling Billy by one of his legs, walked into the girls' toilets, and, giggling a little, held him over the sink. She turned the tap on full and watched the struggling spider going round and round as the water gurgled down the plughole.

"That's got rid of him," thought Jane with satisfaction. "Serves him right anyway."

At registration Jane looked all round the classroom, but Billy wasn't there. She began to feel uneasy. Surely she had gone too far this time. But just then there was a deafening wail and Billy Briggs burst into the room, dripping wet and sobbing. The class roared with laughter. Billy really was a sight!

"It was her. It was Jane Adams that did it!" Billy bawled.

"Don't be silly, Billy!" snapped Miss Prigg. "Jane's been here for the last ten minutes. You'll have to think of a better excuse than that for being late. I think you'd better explain yourself to the headmaster."

And she ushered him out of the room at arm's length.

Ten minutes later a grim-faced Miss Prigg arrived back in the classroom. "Come along, Jane, the headmaster wants to see you immediately," she said sharply. There was no chance to escape. Miss Prigg escorted Jane all the way to the headmaster's office, and even knocked on the heavy wooden door. What could she do? It was too late now.

The headmaster was looking at her in a most curious manner, while Billy Briggs stood in the corner sobbing. He was making a terrible mess of the head's new carpet.

"Now, Jane, what's all this about?" said the headmaster. He sounded quite annoyed. Jane looked around desperately. What could she possibly say?

"Oh heck," thought Jane. "How am I going to get out of this one? I wish I wasn't here."

Then all of a sudden . . .

SHE WASN'T.

Barbara Paterson

Beach:Late Afternoon

Picture by
John Thompson-Steinkrauss

Smooth pebbles lie like lozenges
Waiting for the waves to suck them.
Behind the narrow bank of shingle,
Empty shells of upturned boats
Hide from the tide.
A cold wind blows.

Perched on a flimsy stool
A solitary fisherman sits
Bound to the blue-black water
By a hair-thin line.

Boots scrunch over stones:
A brother angler. He calls—
Voice raised against the rolling waves—
"I've come to drown
My last few worms."

Clouds gather over the dark figures
On the empty beach:
Over the empty, teeming sea.

Very, very, ve

OLD

P
Jose

(a) *City Gent*: "My man, how many calves' tails would be needed to reach from here to the sky?"
Countryman: "One. If it's long enough."

(c) An Oxford don was told that one of a pair of twins who had been students of his had been killed in a road accident. One day, walking in the High, he saw the other brother, rushed up to him and cried:
"Tell me, was it you or your brother who died?"

(b) *Pat*: "Mike, why are you carrying that brick?"
Mike: "I'm trying to sell my house and I'm using it as a sample."

(d) When a cock crows at daybreak, why does it lift one leg up?
—Because if it lifted both legs up it would fall flat on its face.

y, very
ery, very

ɔKɐ8

by
right

These may not be hilariously funny jokes but they have one thing in common. They are all at least *one thousand years old*.

(e) Mike was walking along the road, carrying six eggs in a bag, when he met Pat.

"Hello, Mike," said Pat, "and what have you got in that bag there?"

"Guess!" said Mike. "And if you guess right I'll give you three of them to make an omelet!"

"It's a hard question, that it is," said Pat, wrinkling his forehead. "Could you give me a clue?"

"They're white outside and yellow inside."

"Got it," cried Pat. "They're turnips hollowed out and stuffed with carrots!"

Nobody knows where jokes like these came from, or who first made them up, but learned gentlemen collected them and wrote them down from very early days. All these five jokes were almost certainly told by Arabs in the Middle East and Ancient Greeks. They appeared in the following collections of current witticisms:

(a) *Demands Joyous*, published in 1500 but really a collection of the jokes which the ancient world and the continent had enjoyed.

(b) Hierocles of Alexandria compiled a list of the twenty-one best jokes of the fifth century A.D. This was one.

(c) Hierocles again. Fifth century. One of the oldest jokes in the world.

(d) Mentioned by Bar Hebraeus, leader of the Christians of Syria in the twelfth century, but going back much farther. Certainly a joke enjoyed by the Ancient Greeks.

(e) One of a whole collection of Arabic jokes, put down for the first time in the eleventh century, about a kind of absent-minded professor called So Djoh, who was logical but not very bright.

Brian Ball
A Postcard from the Stars

Illustrated by
Peter Wingham

"What are you going to do with that pile of junk?" Liam called when his brother got back from the scrap-yard with the old Lambretta.

"Rebuild it like new," said Jack proudly. Then he glared at Liam. "And if you lay a finger on it, you'll need rebuilding!"

"I bet they paid you to take it away," Liam shouted from the safety of the fence. "Who'd want to play with that prehistoric wreck!"

He did, of course, so when everyone had gone to bed he put on his dressing-gown and borrowed Jack's gauntlets and crash-helmet and crept out into the garden and sat on the Lambretta.

It was very quiet out there, very quiet and very dark.

"Waaaaarrrrr-waaaaarrrrr—thrummmm!" Liam murmured softly as he took the lead in the Manx Grand Prix. "Pooooowwwwwww-www—Zzzzowwwwwww—Gggggggrrmmm-mmmggggggg!"

He was changing gear for the tight bend before the home straight.

"Zzzzowwwwwww!" he whispered.

"Ggrukk," something answered.

Liam almost leapt off the seat.

"I didn't say that!"

"Ggrukkk," it went again.

"I didn't say that either!"

But something had!

Liam's hair began to stand up straight under the crash-helmet, and he could feel little prickles down his back. He wanted to jump off the Lambretta and make a run for his warm bed, but he didn't dare move.

What if the thing that went "Ggrukk!" was waiting for him?

What if it saw him as he ran for the kitchen?

"I'm not moving!" Liam whispered to himself. "I'll sit here till I'm sure it's gone, then I'll run like an Olympic champion for the back door and maybe it won't get me!"

So Liam sat very still and he waited.

And he waited.

And he waited some more.

"It's gone," he told himself.

He listened again.

"Has it gone?"

He was just about to jump off the old motor-scooter and hare for the kitchen when a metallic sort of grumpy noise went "Grukkk!"

"It's there again!" Liam said to himself. "I wish I was in bed! I wish I hadn't come out to see Jack's rotten old scooter! I wish I hadn't sat on it! I wish I hadn't started yelling 'Warrrrthrummmm' and all those other daft noises!"

He wished so hard he almost thought he hadn't done any of these things, and he was so good at wishing they hadn't happened that he thought he really was back in his own room, at least until something else happened to tell him he wasn't.

And what happened was this:

Behind him—yes, exactly behind him, and

a bit below where he was sitting—something went "Grunkk".

"Oooohh!" Liam cried out aloud.

"Grukkk!" went the noise behind him again, and this time the motor-scooter shook a little—just a little, but enough for Liam to know that there definitely was something behind him, and a little below him.

"It's here!" wailed Liam. "It's in the Lambretta!"

"Gress grri grram!" it answered.

"It's a ghost!" Liam wailed.

"Grro grri'm grrot," it said.

"It's a ghost with a cold!" wailed Liam.

"Grri'm grrot a ghrosstt!" it said impatiently.

"It's a ghost with a cold and it's right behind me," said Liam, who was badly scared, though he wasn't too scared to ask himself what sort of a ghost with a cold went out haunting people on old motor-scooters.

So, though he was scared, he looked around, where, down below him, was the engine, right under the seat of the Lambretta, and the engine was glowing with an odd sort of pearly glow!

"It's in the engine!" Liam said. "It's a ghost with a bad cold right in our Jack's old scooter. What's it doing there?"

"Grrying gro gggret groutt!" it answered in a very angry tone of voice.

"Grying gro grret groutt?" Liam repeated. "Ggrying gro gret groutt? What sort of talk is that?"

"Ggrenglish!" it yelled.

"Ggrenglish?" pondered Liam. "Grott's Ggrenglish?" Then he understood, because he was talking in the same way as the ghost. "You're talking English with too many g's, ghostie!" he said. "Anyway, what are you doing down there?"

"Ggrying gro gret groutt!"

"I know!" said Liam. "Trying to get out. You must be stuck in the sump, ghostie. I'll get some oil and maybe that'll ease your throat a bit. Hang around!"

Liam was still a bit scared, but he was too interested to run for the kitchen now and miss the fun. He couldn't be scared of a ghost who was stuck in an old scooter, could he?

No, he told himself, he couldn't.

He poured oil into the engine, and the pearly glow increased.

"How are you doing in there?" he said. "Feel better, ghostie?"

There was a long oily gurgling sound.

"Ah. Aah! Better. Better and better! And don't call me ghostie, I'm not a ghost."

"Well, what are you?" asked Liam.

"I'm what I suppose you'd call an alien, since I'm not from your planet," the creature, or whatever it was, said.

"Get off with you," said Liam faintly. He only said it because his mother said "Get off with you" when she was feeling peculiar. "You can't be an alien. Aliens don't live in old Lambretta engines."

"It isn't my usual abode, I agree. But since my starship crashed on your planet—"

"—what!" interrupted Liam.

"I said, since my starship crashed near here and was taken to a junkyard and crushed up for scrap, I've had to survive wherever I can."

"In an engine?" said Liam.

"That's where we live," said the creature. "Right amongst the explosions. We're most comfortable where it's hot and cramped and where there's a lot of noise. I needed a place to live when my starship went for scrap, so I transferred to this contraption when they brought it to the junkyard, and there I stayed, getting colder every day, until that brother of yours bought the Lambretta and brought it back here."

"How much did Jack pay?" said Liam.

"Five pounds!" growled the creature, and its pearly glow went red. "Five pounds for an old motor-scooter and for me, Grok of the famous race of Grokkles!"

Liam's head was spinning. He wasn't afraid any more but how could he explain to Jack, or to his mum, that the Lambretta contained a stranded star-traveller who glowed in the dark and was called Grok?

"I don't know what we're going to do about this, Grok," he said. "Can't you come out of there?"

"No!" said Grok. "Grokkles live in engines! We thrive best in a nice warm million-degree fission engine, but even an ancient relic like this is better than nothing, and the sooner this one starts up, the sooner I can get away!"

"But where to?" said Liam. "You won't get far on this old wreck."

"This old wreck can take us right back to my home star, Grokkle-Bright," said Grok. "Just pass me the Lambretta manual and fill up the tank, and I'll show you a thing or two!"

"Will you?" said Liam.

"Sure!" Grok told him.

"Like what?" said Liam.

"Like a tour round a couple of galaxies," said Grok.

"On Jack's Lambretta?"

"Sure!"

Liam laughed with amazement and delight. The Manx Grand Prix could manage without him now.

"O.K., Grok!"

In a couple of minutes, Grok glowed blue then red then pearly-white while he studied the Lambretta manual, as Liam filled the tank with the petrol-and-oil mixture.

"Ready?" said Liam.

"Nearly," Grok told him.

"How do we get out into space?" said Liam.

"Just a minute," said Grok.

Liam looked back at the house, wondering if he had been missed yet.

"Are you sure about trips round galaxies on the Lambretta?" he asked nervously.

"Give me time," said Grok.

But there wasn't any more time.

From the bedroom over the kitchen came a huge yell.

"Where's Liam!" bellowed Jack.

"What's that noise?" said Grok.

"Jack," said Liam faintly. "He's gone to bed."

"Does he always bellow like that in bed?" said Grok.

"Only when he's mad with me," said Liam.

"Aaaargh!" bellowed Jack. "I'll demolish him!"

"Oh," moaned Liam.

"Be quiet!" said Grok.

"Hurry up!" Liam yelled.

The back door burst open, and the garden was suddenly full of bright light.

"There he is!" bawled Jack. "He's on my Lambretta! And he's got my gear on!"

"Careful, Liam," warned Liam's mum. "Jack isn't very pleased with you."

"What do we do now?" moaned Liam.

"Kick the kick-start," said Grok.

Jack was rushing towards him, though, and Liam was too terrified to move, and if Jack hadn't fallen over the oilcan where Liam had left it on the grass, Jack might really have carried out his threat, and then Liam would never have got the Lambretta to start, but Jack *did* fall—very heavily!

"What are you doing, Jack?" called his mother.

"Falling down!" roared Jack.

Liam breathed a sigh of relief and kicked the kick-start.

The old Lambretta roared into louder life than it had ever done before, and Jack said later that it sounded more like a rocket engine than a motor-scooter.

"Off we go," said Grok. "Into gear!"

Liam snapped the gear-lever.

"Powwwwww—zoooommmmmmm!" howled the Lambretta.

"Where to?" yelled Liam above the noise.

A flash of moonlight came from behind the clouds.

"Straight up the moonbeam," said Grok.

So Liam pointed the Lambretta for the moonlight, and to the absolute astonishment of Jack, and Jack's mum, and his dad, who had just come out to see what all the noise was about, Liam and the Lambretta zoomed up into the sky along a bright, white moonbeam with a noise like an interstellar ship.

"What's that boy up to now?" said Liam's dad.

"I'll send you a postcard!" Liam called down to his family. "'Bye!"

"A postcard?" said Liam's dad. "He'll have a job getting it delivered from up there."

Liam's mum thought otherwise.

"Liam always keeps his promises," she said. "If he says he'll send a postcard, he'll send it."

So Liam's mum and dad, and Jack too, now that he'd got over losing his Lambretta, watched the sky every night, and after a week they saw what they were looking for.

In the gap between the constellations of Orion and the Pleiades, a new set of stars had appeared, and together they spelt out a message:

Having a lovely time wish you were here back soon love Liam

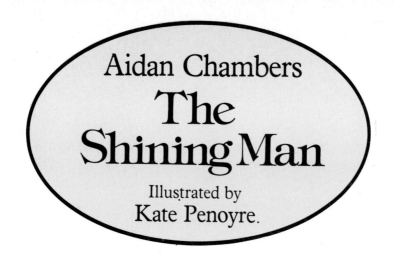

Aidan Chambers
The Shining Man

Illustrated by
Kate Penoyre.

Once long ago there was a mighty hunter. He had a large family and they lived in their wigwam on the edge of the forest.

All day long the hunter's children played in the forest or wandered on the prairie. At night they came home to see what their father had caught for them to eat.

Though he was a mighty hunter, their father often returned empty-handed. In the summer his family could find berries to eat. But in the winter there was nothing, and so the children went to bed hungry.

That was the way of things. The children did not complain, but being hungry made them unhappy.

When the time came for the hunter's eldest son to become a man, his father sent him away on his own.

"You must find your own food," his father told him. "And build your own shelter. Your courage will be tested. If you live and become a man, you will return. And then you will hunt with me."

The boy set out, taking with him enough food for three days, but nothing more.

For three days he walked deep into the forest. On the fourth day he came suddenly upon a wide and pleasant glade.

"I will stop here," the boy said to himself, "and build a shelter. After that I will rest, and then I will search for food."

So he gathered some leafy branches blown from trees and made a wigwam. Inside, he spread a carpet of moss and laid a bed of grass upon it.

That night he slept well. His bed was warm and soft and he was tired from his long trek.

Next day he searched for food, but he found nothing.

He searched the next day. Again he found nothing.

And the third day.

That night he was weary, and very hungry.

"I will pray to the Great Spirit," he said. "I will pray to be brave and strong, and that I become a man. The Great Spirit will help me."

He thought of asking for food. "But," he said to himself, "that would be a gift for myself alone. I will ask for something that will help everyone."

And so he prayed, and that night he fell asleep where he prayed, huddled by a fire he had made to keep his starving body warm.

In the middle of the darkness he was suddenly woken. A bright light shone in his eyes. The light was not from his fire. The flames had died as he slept. And it was not from the moon for the clouds covered the sky. The light came from a shining figure standing near him.

The figure was like a man dressed in flowing green clothes. On his head was a plume of shining golden feathers.

"Who are you?" asked the boy, startled.

"I come from the Great Spirit," the shining figure said. "He will answer your prayers. But you must promise to do whatever I ask."

"What must I do?" asked the boy.

"I will tell you when I come again," the man said. "First you must promise."

The boy was afraid and weak and sleepy. But he remembered his father's warning. His courage would be tested. He must not fail.

"I promise," he said.

Immediately, the shining man disappeared.

Next morning, the boy searched harder than ever for food. Still he found nothing. And when darkness came he lay down exhausted.

The shining man woke him in the middle of the night. "Are you ready?" he asked.

The boy's body was weak but his courage was strong. He rose and stood before the gleaming figure. "Ready," he said.

"Wrestle with me," said the man.

Man and boy wrestled together. They tussled and twisted and tugged. They lunged and tugged at each other. And to his surprise, the boy found he could fight well. But he could not throw the shining man to the ground.

Next night they fought again. And the next. And the next.

And every night the boy found he was growing stronger while the shining man was growing weaker. He did not know why; but it was so.

The seventh night of their wrestling came. The man appeared. But now his green clothes were torn and his golden plume of feathers drooped about his head. He shone no more.

"Tonight," he said, "you shall win. I shall die."

"Die!" the boy said. "How can that be?"

"Do not question," the man said. "Only obey, as you promised. When I am dead you must take off my green clothes. You must take off my golden plume. You must bury me in the earth. You must leave here. But you must not forget me. And one day you must come back and tend my grave."

The boy was deeply sad. "Must I do this?" he asked.

"The Great Spirit commands it," said the man. "Now wrestle with me."

So they fought all night long. And as morning dawned the green man died.

Carefully, the boy stripped him of his tattered green clothes and his faded golden feathers. Then he buried the man deep in the softest earth of the pleasant glade.

Next day the boy set off for home, eager to see his father again. And his father welcomed him with joy.

"You have survived," he said, full of pride. "Now you are a man."

And every day afterwards father and son went hunting together.

But the boy did not forget the shining figure. He remembered each evening when he prayed to the Great Spirit, and he waited for the day to come when it would be time to visit the shining man's grave.

Soon the spring arrived. The trees burst into fresh green. The new grass on the prairie rippled in the wind like waves on the great lake. And then the boy knew his time had come to return to the pleasant glade.

He soon found the place again, and it was so beautiful that he wondered how he could ever have left it. The ground where the shining man was buried was the loveliest of all. There, delicate green shoots were growing and the silence was a special kind of music.

Time and again that summer, the boy visited the grave and tended it, keeping it free of all but the delicate green shoots growing there. They grew and grew and filled him with wonder at the change that slowly came upon them.

Then one day he came running from the forest.

"Father, father," he called, "come with me. Hurry, I have something marvellous to show you."

His father followed him back into the forest. And there he saw that over the place that had been the shining man's grave tall plants were growing, higher than his head. On their long thin stems were great golden heads of grain, rich and ripe and succulent.

The hunter raised his hands to the sky.

"This is what the Great Spirit promised long ago," he said. "He has sent us the corn of the Good Spirit."

"It is a gift for everyone," the boy said. "The Great Spirit has answered my prayer. I thank him!"

There and then father and son danced and sang their praise.

The shining stranger had returned.

Ron and Atie van der Meer

A NIGHT OUT

"I don't feel like going to bingo, Ethel. Can't we do something different tonight?"
"I know! Why not burgle a house for a change, Hilda?"

"We'll look just like ordinary burglars with this outfit, Ethel."
"You're right, Hilda. We don't want the neighbours to recognise us, do we?"

"This seems a nice house to burgle."
"Mmm, I don't like the curtains much."

"Hilda, I can't get my arm out!"

"Now look what you've done, Ethel! You've ruined the door and nearly broken my arm."
"Don't make such a fuss, Hilda. We've got a job to do. Let's try that window."

"Hurry up, Hilda . . . Oh blast, my foot's stuck. Do something!"

"Ethel, someone's coming. What do we do?"
"Quick, hold your breath and pretend to be a statue!"

"I must be dreaming."

"Phew, that was close! Let's go home. I've had enough."
"I hope you've got the keys, Hilda."

"No, but I left the kitchen window open!"
"Help! Get me the police! WE'VE BEEN BURGLED!"

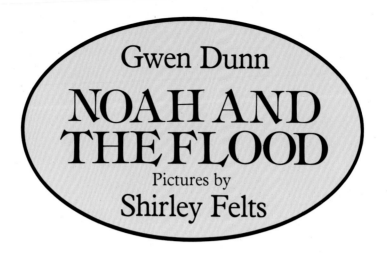

Gwen Dunn

NOAH AND THE FLOOD

Pictures by
Shirley Felts

Somehow the animals understood before the
people.
From the forests first came the great ones,
secretly, in pairs
Leaving all their kind behind.
The giraffes, as always, gave themselves airs
And hedgehogs rolled up out of fear
And squeaked, "It's not us! We aren't here!"
Squash-footed, swing-headed elephants came
together
Quietly talking about the forecast weather.
Great cats and the dogs looking sideways at
them
Purred. Furred.
Tiger at wolf, leopard at jackal, cheetah
At fox. Long smile never neater.
Though he and his mate
Left cubs—all russet eight,
Tuggety-ruggety rolling around,
Not expecting to be drowned.

The earth then whispered with the busy
hurry
Of all the little creatures in a secret flurry
To be away from something—what, they did
not know—
They understood only—the two spiders, two
ants, two all—that they must go.

And like an idiot chorus came the pairs
Of monkeys and apes
Giving penny armchairs
And playing japes,
Chit-chattering, gossiping, cheeking the
baboons.
Loons
With round, sad eyes.
Perhaps they were wise
And played the fool to forget
The full forests of friends they left
Which soon would be
of all living creatures utterly bereft.

And then:

Down came the rain
A steely grill
To fill
The space between sky and earth,
A colour dearth
Nothing but grey
All day
Every day
Day after day after day
For five times eight
Wet days the spate
Of water rose
Against those
Who hadn't believed Jaweh, the god,
And thought Noah was just odd.

Then came terror!

"Save us! Save us! Save us!
Take us aboard!
We'll worship your lord.
We want to die old
We'll do as we're told!"

The people cried
And tried
To hide
In trees or flimsy boats
Or floats
Made of bark
Not firm and weatherproof like the ark.

"Save us, Noah, please do!
Let us come too.
We'll be good as gold
Let us live to be old!"

People guffawed. There were gales of
    laughter
When the animals came
And the days after
"That fool Noah and his sons the same!"

They lay time-wasting in the sun
(Some did things worse).
They didn't believe in god's curse
Nor rain nor flood
Nor anything sad
Or bad
Because
Well—that's how the world was.

Then it began to rain
The straight rain out of the high sky
Never before seen. Never seen again.
And none could understand why
Suddenly the earth, comfortably dry
Till then, should be spotted wet.
None took much notice—not yet.

Tip tap, pit pat, tip tap, pit pat
Tip tap, pit, pat, tip tap, pitty pat
Drops into blots
Blots into blobs
Blobs into splodges
Into runnels, funnels of streaming rain
Streams into lakes into seas
And everyone went indoors to get dry and
     sneeze.

And the rain fell splish splosh
Till the world was awash
And Noah with all his family
Floated quite safely
As god had said they would
Because they'd been good.
And the animals grew thin and lank
And everything—even the butterflies—
     stank.

And Noah's wife shut her ears to the sad
    outside calling
And fed chimps, cats, dogs and even fleas to
    stop them bawling!
Swish went the rain
Day after long day
Of grey
Until waking after sleep was full of dread
And Noah's wife wished quite sincerely that
    she was dead.

One morning, grey as the others—no, not
    quite,
The birds whispered and fluttered
Small beasts after long silence muttered
"It's getting light!"
The monkeys played again,
The cock crowed at the hen,
Great cats and great dogs,
Elephant, deer and hogs
Snuffed up air in a new way
And blundered on deck to see and stay.
Noah, Japhet, Shem and Ham
Listened.
Everything still glistened
Wet, but undimpled,
The smooth water was not pimpled with rain.
They stared again
And knew
What was true.
Croaking for joy, the frog hopped
Overboard. The rain had stopped.

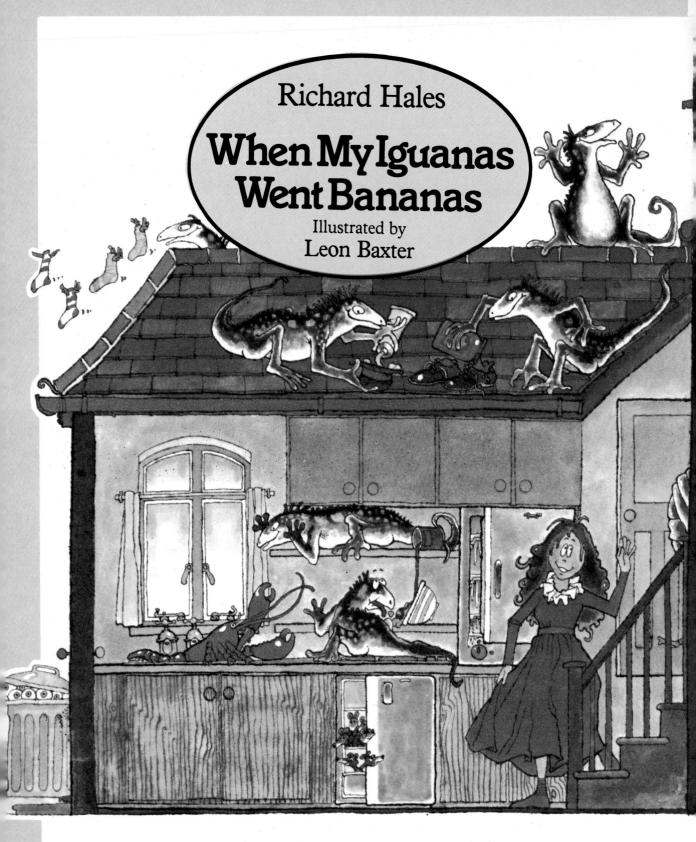

Richard Hales

When My Iguanas Went Bananas

Illustrated by
Leon Baxter

There was curry in my custard
There was jam inside my shoe
My socks had all migrated
And my hat was full of glue

When my iguanas went bananas . . .

There were spiders in the bathroom
Although that's nothing new
They all had knives and forks
And were eating people-stew

When my iguanas went bananas . . .

There were icicles in the oven
And the postman bit our dog
And a lumberjack came floating
Through our front door on a log

When my iguanas went bananas . . .

My trousers started shrinking
And the fridge was full of mice
There was a lobster in the kitchen sink
And my sister turned quite nice

When my iguanas went bananas . . .

There were bloodstains on the carpet
And dead men behind the telly
There were footprints on the ceiling
And my bed was full of jelly

When my iguanas went bananas . . .

The dustbin was full of eyeballs
I WAS BEING DEVOURED BY A
  GIANT FLEA!
Why does my imagination
Play such silly tricks on me?

When my iguanas went bananas . . .

CLOTHES
By
QUENTIN BELL

Three hundred years ago there were no children. Children were invented about a hundred years later.

The above statement is untrue and quite ridiculous. Nevertheless there is a *kind* of truth about it. For although children got born in very great quantities three hundred years ago—and died in almost equally great quantities, I am sorry to say—their parents did not think of them as "children" in quite the way that modern parents do; as people who have rather different ideas from grown-ups and who like different things.

Our ancestors gave their children beer for breakfast. And expected them to read long and difficult books written by, and for, grown-ups. They were thought of as small, ignorant adults and if they did not behave in an adult fashion they were brutally and continually beaten. Children of noble or rich parents were part of their parents' wealth; they were pawns in a game of power and had to marry who their parents chose for them so that the parents could acquire more land by the union.

Not only were the children of past centuries treated as miniature adults but they were also dressed like miniature adults. This was particularly true of noble and royal children as paintings of the period show. The picture on the opposite page is a sketch of a famous portrait painted by Largillière of James Stuart, the Young Pretender, and his sister Louisa Maria Theresa. They were probably dressed up a bit for their portrait but these would have been very much the kind of clothes they had to wear all day.

Louisa is dressed almost exactly as her mother would have been dressed. She is encased in a stiff, tight bodice of white satin and fine lace. There is a great deal more lace on the front of her skirt and she wears a long train that will drag along the ground as she walks, picking up all sorts of dirt and grease (the floors were usually exceedingly dirty, even in palaces). Stuck on top of her head is more lace, elaborately made up into what was called a *fontages*, a headdress which was very fashionable about the year 1690.

James is crammed into a doublet embroidered with much gold and ornamented with lots of buttons and frogged button holes. I doubt whether he ever would, or indeed could, actually do up all the buttons. Beneath the doublet are breeches of matching colour, and beneath the breeches garters and hose and heavy, high-heeled leather shoes. The thing under his arm is an enormous hat trimmed with an enormous feather. Admire his elaborate cravat, which is presumably part of his shirt. The shirt reappears, all frills and fine elegance, at his wrist. Behind him, for all gentlemen and gentlemanly small boys carried them, hung a small but usable sword.

The dog wears a handsome collar ornamented with gold.

Children who wore clothes of this kind were expected to behave perfectly at all times, to move about in a stately fashion, to bow, curtsey, and generally to hang about the place looking decorative. It must have been dreadfully tedious and desperately uncomfortable.

Today, the miniature adults are children, dressed in the sort of clothes they like—loose, airy, comfortable. In all ways better.

Except that a small but usable sword *would* be nice to wear.

Cynthia Mitchell

Animal Tales

Pictures by
Frances Livens

Any branching horn that a stag has worn
Will serve as a wall decoration,
But elk or moose is the type to choose
If you're looking for admiration.

If you're looking for use
On the horns of a moose
Or an elk from Scandinavia,
You can colonise bats or park old hats
And all sorts of paraphernalia.

A yawning hippopotamus
Could swallow quite a lot of us,
So do advise your friends as follows,
KEEP AWAY FROM HIPPO WALLOWS.

A grizzly bear broke into a shack
Where lived a lonely lumberjack;

The lumberjack broke into a run
When the bear made straight for his
hunting gun;

The hunting gun broke into six bits
With just one swipe of the grizzly's mitts;

The lumberjack broke out in a sweat
And as far as I know he's running yet;

But the grizzly's face broke out in a grin
As he pulled up a chair and settled in.

We all look up to the proud giraffe,
He makes such a splendid photograph,

But he ignores us; with disdain
He sniffs the air and makes it plain
That admiration bores him stiff;
He looks as if he's caught a whiff
Of something nasty on the breeze,
Our presence clearly doesn't please.

A pompous beast is the proud giraffe.
I bet you've never seen one laugh!

More Peculiar People
by Jean Kenward and Gillian Chapman

There was a man
of fifty wits
who laughed until
he fell to bits.
He laughed until
he grew so fat
the armchair shivered
where he sat.

He squirmed and giggled
on the floor
and heaved, and hiccupped
more and more.

The tears ran down
his cheek. He wheezed
and groaned and giggled,
snuffed and sneezed.
His waistcoat buttons
popped, and burst—
but worse than that—
yes, quite the worst—

It was when he had
fifty fits
and laughed so much
he fell to bits.

They had to sweep him
in a pan,
and give him to
the dustbin man.

They found his buttons
everywhere
and bits of laughter
here and there . . .

They put his snuffles
in a sack.
I wonder if
he will come back.

I wonder if
he's far, or near,
and what is that
strange noise I hear

That isn't either
near, or far?
Ha ha HA HA
                    HA
                    HA
                    HA HA!

My cousin Mary's
as slim as a fiddle:
a length of elastic
can meet round her middle.

She's got a red jumper
with pockets around it,
and if a thing's lost
you may guess she has found it.

My cousin Mary
is careful and tidy;
she's sweet and she's proper
from Monday to Friday,

she's clean and she's gentle,
she's everything good.
She don't stick her tongue out . . .

I do wish she would.

Barbara Paterson
Henny's Half a Fortune

Illustrated by
Peter Dennis

"You don't get much for 20p these days." Henny gazed longingly at a box of monster peaches sheltering under the warning *Don't Pinch Me 'Til I'm Yours*.

"You get more than you do for nothing," Bruce pointed out. "My dad docked my money this week when one of my shots nearly bust the kitchen window. Wasn't fair, 'cause it didn't."

They wandered on through the market, past pyramids of plaster saints and curly black wigs on poles, stopping to sniff at the Freshly-Roasted Peanuts stall.

"I can't even run to those," said Henny. "I keep waiting for fame and fortune, but I'd like to know when they were going to happen."

"You could always ask the fortune-teller." Bruce nodded towards the small line of people half-hidden behind the old sewing-machines stall. At the front of the queue a skinny woman with a flat mortar board on her long grey hair was bending over the hand of a large man with a tartan cap.

"It's an idea. Have *you* ever had your fortune told?"

"No. Except once when my mum bought some paper flowers off a gipsy, she said I had a lucky face and she saw a change of scene ahead. I don't know about the luck yet, but it was just before we came to live round the corner from you. Go on—have a go!"

Henny started to move across to the young man with the spiky hair and silver jacket who was the only one left waiting. He was shifting uneasily, staring intently at a sewing-machine covered in gold sphinxes.

"Suppose she tells me I'm going to break my leg?" she said. "I'd much rather not know."

"I don't suppose she tells them anything nasty, or no one'd want to see her. Come on—it's only a bit of a lark!"

The silver jacket turned and disappeared behind a screen of saucepans, and the fortune-teller beckoned impatiently.

"Don't dilly-dally! Every moment's precious. Live life to the full. Come along now!"

Henny gulped.

"Please, how much is it?"

"How much is it? Whatever it is it's cheap at the price. A fortune's worth a fortune, wouldn't you say? That's logic, isn't it? How much is it?" she repeated, and bent down to stare intently into Henny's eyes. "How much have you got?" she asked sharply.

"20p."

"20p? 20p? You can't expect much of a fortune for 20p, can you now? Not much of a fortune for that."

"I thought maybe it was half-price for under-sixteens, like on the buses."

"You thought? You weren't thinking at all. Half price on buses is one thing. Half-price fortunes is another. Young ones should be double, not half. Got more fortune to be told, haven't you? Chances are, anyway." She settled her mortar-board more firmly on her head. "Still, seeing as business has dropped

115

off momentarily, I'll do you half a fortune for a knock-down rate of 20p. But keep it to yourself. We don't want half the district queuing up for half a fortune, do we? No, we don't," she answered herself, and took Henny's hand in hers.

She paused for a moment; her fingers felt thin and dry. Then she began to speak in a confidential murmur. Henny had to strain to hear.

"You're not the eldest in your family . . . You're always busy, full of ideas. Sometimes they're good, sometimes not so good. You'll do well, but life won't always be easy. You've a helpful side to your nature—sometimes you get carried away. I see that soon you will find something, lose something, gain something—"

"Hey! Reena!" The young man selling the sewing-machines jerked his head towards the alleyway between the stalls.

The next moment the fortune-teller had vanished, slipping between two rows of shiny dresses.

A policeman strolled past listening to his walkie-talkie.

"What a swiz!" said Henny. "I bet I only got a quarter-fortune!"

"What did she tell you then?"

"I'll find something, lose something, gain something. I ask you! Is that worth 20p?"

"Depends what you find. Supposing it's a diamond necklace? Or—"

"Come off it! Who's going to wear a diamond necklace here? Let alone lose it."

"All right!" said Bruce. "Still, we could keep our eyes open."

They found a button underneath the old clothes stall; a 2p piece beside a litter bin; a pin near the ribbon lady.

"See a pin and pick it up," said Henny hopefully; but the promised good luck failed to materialise.

By the time they reached the West Indian in the red, yellow and green tea cosy hat selling chipped ice topped with bright pink syrup, Henny was loudly bewailing her vanished 20p.

"That's the last time I put a fortune before the things that really matter. Look at that! It makes my mouth water."

"Can't be helped. Let's go down the pet shop and say hello to Melly."

They stopped outside to tickle the guinea pigs through the bars, and walked in past the goldfish and the terrapins to the big domed cage in the middle of the shop.

"Hello, Melly!" said Bruce.

The mynah put his glossy head on one side and stared at them unblinkingly.

"Hello, Melly!" repeated Henny.

Melly jerked his head up.

"Hello, Sunshine!"

A grape rolled from his open beak and rolled by Henny's feet. She bent down to pursue it. It rolled on between two open sacks of wheat and dog biscuits. As she squatted down to retrieve it her fingers felt something solid, squashed in the shadows out of sight.

She sat down on the sawdust-covered floor and reached further between the sacks. She felt something soft—yet hard: almost alive. She prodded.

"*Tell me a story!*"

"That wasn't you, Henny!"

"Course it wasn't! Do I squeak?"

Henny's hand closed round something silky. She tugged. Out shot a very new doll with a waterfall of bright gold hair.

"Hello everyone! It's time for tea!"

"Wish it was," said Bruce. "I'm starving."

"Well, we haven't struck gold," said Henny, "but it looks like we've found Goldilocks instead. Let's look for whoever's lost her."

"Half a pound of tuppeny rice!" chanted Goldilocks. *"Half a pound of treacle!"*

"Positively *no* treacle," said the red-headed assistant, scooping dog biscuits from the sack. "Nor no tuppeny rice neither. What about a bag of barley, eh, darlin'?"

Henny ignored him.

"Come on, Bruce! Let's track down a grateful Granny."

She paused to give Melly back his grape. He took it delicately, and hung upside down, watching them leave with eyes like glistening glass buttons.

Henny held the doll in the crook of her arm. The layers of frilly skirt tickled her elbow.

"Do you think we should say anything?" asked Bruce.

"A bit of a problem. If we shout 'Anyone lost a doll?' we risk getting hordes of kids rushing up."

"But if we don't, how'll anyone know?"

"Tricky."

They walked on broodingly towards what Henny called the backwards auction man.

"I'm going to *give* it away," he shouted enthusiastically, leaning over his china horses and flowery teapots. "I'm going to give it *all* away."

His wife bobbed up from behind the Slightly Second glasses.

"Now who could say fairer than that? Ain't he doing you a favour?"

"I'm not asking £5, not £4, not £3! No! Who'll be the first to offer me £1, ladies? £1—only £1!"

A shrivelled-looking woman pressed forwards, waving a note in the air.

"That's the way the money goes!"

The backwards auction man spun round. So did his wife and the shrivelled woman and the small crowd of onlookers.

Henny clapped her hand over Goldilocks's rosebud lips.

"Pop goes the weasel!" squeaked the voice from under her broad pink sash.

The crowd laughed. The shrivelled woman put her note back in her purse. The man scowled.

Henny and Bruce beat a hasty retreat.

Safely round the corner, they stopped to watch the two men on the stall selling fur oddments. One was small and brown and one was large and bright pink, and both wore fur hats. They were bending intently over a backgammon board, fingers swiftly flicking the counters to and fro.

Henny switched the doll from one arm to the other.

"Come along now!" shrieked Goldilocks. *"Nighty nighty Daddy! Time for beddy-byes!"*

The pink-faced man shot upright and knocked the corner of the board. Counters spilled sideways into a pile of mittens. The small brown man turned angrily towards them.

Henny and Bruce moved rapidly down the side-turning past the 10p mechanical horses.

"Good-morning Mummy! Tell me a story!"

Bruce groaned.

"We're never going to get that all over again! It's worse than next-door's baby."

Henny gazed at the doll with disfavour. It lay back in her arm and shut its spiky eyelashes.

"What next, I wonder?"

What next was a sharp kick on her ankle.

Henny spun round and saw a small plump fair-haired girl with her teeth clenched tight.

The small girl picked up one neat white-socked foot and kicked her again.

"Gimme!" She had a high piercing wail. "Gimme! 'Sesmeralda! I want her back!"

Henny jumped out of reach.

"Do you?" she said. "You certainly won't get her like that!" She bent down and rubbed her ankle.

"Aaaaaaaaah!" screeched the small girl. "'Snot yours! 'Smine!"

She ran forwards and bit Henny sharply on her arm.

"You little—!"

Bruce plucked the small girl out of reach.

"Whatever are you doing with my Susan?" said an angry voice. "And what are you doing with my Susan's Esmeralda? How dare you snatch her? Give her back at once!"

For a moment words failed Henny; but only for a moment.

"Snatch her? We found her in the pet shop where your Susan dropped her, and we've been looking for your Susan ever since. And now your Susan has kicked me twice, and

your Susan has bitten me once, and I wouldn't be seen dead with your Susan's Esmeralda! And if I ever *did* have your Susan's Esmeralda, I wouldn't dress her up to look like an outsize meringue, I can tell you!"

The corset lady on the corset stall chuckled.

The fishmonger said; "That's right, girl! You stand up for yourself!"

Susan's mother turned bright scarlet.

"A meringue, eh?" said the corset lady. "More like a cream split, I'd say!"

Susan's mother choked.

Henny looked: and suddenly light dawned.

Susan was wearing the same white frilly skirts as Esmeralda, and the same frilly top, and the same pink sash.

Henny held out the doll.

"You're welcome," she said stiffly, "to have your Esmeralda back."

Susan's mother scuffled around in her handbag. Pointedly not looking at the grinning faces surrounding her, she handed Henny a note.

"Thank you," she said, forcing out the words. "And I'm sorry Susan bit you."

She did not, actually, sound sorry at all; and Susan stuck her tongue out behind her mother's back; but Henny, slipping the pound into the pocket of her jeans, only smiled in reply.

"I don't know what you can expect for half a fortune," she said to Bruce, as they started to retrace their steps. "But she did get it partly right. I did find something. And I gained something. But as for the lost bit—"

"She was right there too!" said Bruce.

"How d'you mean? What did I lose?"

Bruce laughed.

"You should have seen your face! Your temper, of course!"

Henny punched him in the ribs.

"Maybe I'll run to a whole fortune next time! So what's it to be? Chips? Or ice cream? No! Both!"

What-a-Mess
and his
Half Birthday
by
Frank Muir

Illustrated by Joseph Wright.

Prince Amir of Kinjan, noble Afghan hound puppy, otherwise known as What-a-Mess because his coat was always entangled with such un-noble rubbish as sump-oil, bits of eggshell, twigs, jam, clods of earth, paint and sticky-buds, woke up, opened one eye and—most unusual, this—climbed straight out of his basket and barked a short greeting to the morning.

He had suddenly remembered that this was his (half) birthday! "Today," he said to himself proudly, "I am (almost) grown up. I am *six months old*!"

He felt sure that the family who lived in his house would want to greet him on his (half) birthday morn so he decided to tidy himself up before making an entrance.

The back corridor was a bit smelly because the man had painted it the previous evening and the paint was not quite dry but What-a-Mess held his breath and de-messed his coat by shaking himself vigorously from nose to tail, as his mother had taught him to do that day he had fallen into the canal. Bits of paint, eggshell, twigs, etc., flew off his coat like bullets and stuck to the wet paint on the walls. He was pleased about this because the family were always grumbling that he made the floor dirty.

The family were having breakfast in the kitchen. He decided to give them a nice surprise by entering unseen and then, with a lithe Afghan leap, landing lightly in the middle of the breakfast table. Where they could all congratulate him on being such an old and beautiful puppy.

It did not happen quite like that.

He leapt lithely but when he landed on the tablecloth he kept going, taking the tablecloth with him on to the floor.

It was very exciting. Cups of tea were flung all over the place. The man ended up on his back in the fireplace with porridge all over his shirt and the lady had her elbow in the marmalade.

Everybody was shouting his name—except the man, who was shouting names What-a-Mess had never heard before—so he knew his entrance had been a success. Barking with pleasure, he raced out into the garden and fell in a heap in his Number Three Top-Secret Hiding-Place, a hollow he had made in a huge pile of rotting lawn-mowings.

It was a lovely day. The sun was hot and getting hotter and What-a-Mess decided to celebrate his semi-anniversary by making lists of everything he had ever learned during the whole of his long puppy life.

What I Love Most in the World

   My mother
   Scratching behind my ear
   The string from the Sunday roast beef
   Having my tummy rubbed
   Barking at butterflies
   Sleeping
   Creeping up behind people and surprising them with my nose

What I Hate Most in the World
   Dustmen
   Worm pills
   Being bathed
   Having a paw trodden on
   Dog biscuits
   Other animals in my garden
   Going in the car to the vet

My Favourite Food
   Coal
   The glue on envelopes
   Catfood
   All human food,
   particularly if left on the edge of a plate
   Chamois leather
   Plastic containers
   Radio Times

My Worst Enemy
   The cat-next-door (she is a bit younger than me and is quick and I
     never seem to win)

My Best Friend
   The cat-next-door (well, she is there and we muck about a lot in
     the garden and play games)

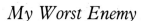

My Worst Fault
    Haven't got one

My Resolution to Make Myself a Better Dog
    I do hereby swear that for the rest of my life, puppy and dog, I
    will try to stay awake and not fall asleep in the middle of . . .

That was as far as What-a-Mess got. He had suddenly fallen asleep.

Read All About Us

Brian Ball lives in Doncaster and writes about cats, notably a cool cat called Jackson (*Jackson's House*, published by Hamish Hamilton, and three more). He also writes about flying saucers (*A Young Person's Guide to UFOs*, published by Granada).

Leon Baxter is a freelance graphic designer who has worked a lot for advertising and for educational publications. He has two children and a parrot and is particularly fond of drawing chunks of machinery, such as steamrollers.

Quentin Bell is Emeritus Professor of the History and Theory of Art, Sussex University. He is also a painter, sculptor, potter, art critic, and the author of many books, one of which is on a similar theme to the piece he has written and painted for us. It is called *On Human Finery*, and is published by the Hogarth Press.

Quentin Blake is Head of the Department of Illustration at the Royal College of Art. He is also one of our most prolific and successful freelance illustrators. Three more examples of his work, out of a great many in the bookshops, are *The Wild Washerwomen* (story by John Yeoman), published by Hamish Hamilton; *Mr Magnolia*, published by Jonathan Cape; and *The Puffin Book of Improbable Records*.

Michael Bond began writing in the army, mainly to alleviate the boredom of life in an Egyptian tent. He was for many years a cameraman for BBC Television then, in 1958, he published a book for children with the title of *A Bear Called Paddington*. The rest, as they say, is history! Besides writing about Paddington he also writes stories about Olga da Polga, a mouse called Thursday, and an armadillo called J.D. Polson.

Michelle Cartlidge writes and draws picture books. Sometimes about mice (*Pippin and Pod* and *A Mouse's Diary*) and sometimes about bears (*The Bears' Bazaar* and *Teddy Trucks*). Her publisher is Heinemann. She draws all her drawings on location in Hampstead where she lives. She so enjoyed doing the working mice for us that she is now hard at work on a whole book of them to be called *Mousework*.

Sir Hugh Casson, KCVO, is President of the Royal Academy. He is really an architect but he so loves painting water-colours that he may be found at any spare minute with a paintbox in his hand and a brush in his teeth. He has published a number of books (full of water-colour paintings) including *The Old Man of Lochnagar* (story written by H.R.H. The Prince of Wales) published by Hamish Hamilton.

Margaret Chamberlain graduated from the Royal College of Art in 1979 and has since illustrated several children's books. She lives in London and likes knitting, making clothes, cooking and eating.

Aidan Chambers taught for eleven years, was a monk for seven, and has been a full-time writer for fourteen, during which time he has written thirty-six books, including the anthologies *Funny Folk*, *Ghost Carnival* and *Animal Fair*, which are published by Heinemann. Recently he presented a series on children's books, *Long, Short and Tall Stories* on BBC TV.

Gillian Chapman has been a full time illustrator of books since she left Harrow School of Art. One of them, *Clutterby Hogg*, published by Frederick Warne, is a picture story book written by Jean Kenward (q.v.). Apart from illustrating she also likes tapestry, embroidery, knitting and lacemaking.

Peter Cross, who drew our cover as well as *Rush-hour at Fittlethorpe Halt*, qualified as an illustrator at Hawker Siddeley, drawing aircraft and bits of machinery. He has spent the last five years working on his own children's book, written by Peter Dallas Smith, which is to be published by Ernest Benn.

Peter Dennis has illustrated Barbara Paterson's collection of stories *Henny Takes a Hand*, published by Hippo, and lots of other things. When questioned he confessed that his interests are military history, playing with toy soldiers and murdering the lute.

Craig Dodd not only designs books, but writes them as well. They include the lively *Young Person's Guide to Ballet* published by MacDonald.

Gwen Dunn decided in 1939 that it was risky for somebody without a winter coat to "write" for a living so became a teacher. However, her pupils over the years, whose ages ranged from 3 to 57, allowed her to write and broadcast about them, and for them, and taught her a great deal. Two of her books are *Simon's Last Year*, published by Methuen, and *The Box in the Corner*, published by Macmillan.

Philip Ennis writes poems and articles about the countryside of Rutland, where he lives. He teaches at a large comprehensive school and is also a magistrate.

Shirley Felts was born in West Virginia, USA. Her husband is an architect and they spent a year and a half travelling through Asia and the Middle East, sketching. Exhibitions of her work have been held in England and America, and she has illustrated many children's books.

Richard Hales is a young teacher. He tells us that his chief interest is inflicting stories, poems and his excruciating sense of humour on captive and unsuspecting children, under the guise of "English" lessons.

Colin Hawkins is a young illustrator who specialises in drawing funny pictures. Two of the books he wrote and illustrated are *Father Christmas and his Friends*, with Chris Maynard, published by W.H. Allen, and *The Witches*, published by Granada.

Hans Helweg was born in Denmark and worked on farms there as a young man. He is an amateur naturalist and likes anything to do with wood, be it making things with it, chopping it, or splitting it. During the war he joined the American forces and was in the ski troops, which was not easy for him as he had no idea how to ski. He has illustrated all the Olga da Polga books by Michael Bond, has recently had a series of four animal books published by Collins and is responsible for *The Travels of Oggy, Oggy at Home*, and *Oggy and the Holiday*, all published by Gollancz and, in paperback, Pan Books.

Christopher Hood lives in a cramped house in the Rhondda Valley with his wife, three children, two dogs, a cat and a budgerigar. His interests are writing, reading, painting, and lying in bed. He also talks a great deal but people usually ignore him. This is his first story for children.

Faith Jaques has written and illustrated two picture books about Tilly, *Tilly's House* and *Tilly's Rescue*, both published by Heinemann. She is a very distinguished and well-known illustrator who has illustrated something like a hundred books. Among them are Alison Uttley's *Tales of Little Grey Rabbit* (Heinemann), Leon Garfield's *Apprentice* stories (Heinemann), and Roald Dahl's *Charlie and the Chocolate Factory* (Allen and Unwin, and Puffin).

Jean Kenward is married, lives in Chorleywood, Bucks, and has a grownup family. She is a part-time lecturer in Complementary Studies at Harrow College of Higher Education. Her poetry, songs and stories are broadcast in BBC Schools Programmes and her work for adults and children appears in anthologies.

Priscilla Lamont has illustrated Harry Secombe's *Katy and the Nurgla* (Robson Books and Puffin). She trained at Canterbury College of Art and later spent a year in South America. She is a keen sailor and paints portraits as well as illustrating books.

Penelope Lively lives in a 17th-century house in a village in Oxfordshire, a part of the country she likes to write about. Her many books for children include *The Ghost of Thomas Kempe*, *Astercote*, *The Voyage of QV66* and *The Revenge of Samuel Stokes*; they are all published by Heinemann, and most of them in paperback by Piccolo.

Frances Livens is a portrait painter who has painted many famous stars of theatre and cinema. She has also run an art gallery, but has lately turned to illustration.

Eunice and Nigel McMullen are both teachers. Eunice works as a teacher and librarian and Nigel as an art teacher and freelance illustrator. They jointly produce *Bookworm*, a children's magazine about books. *Just Imagine* arose out of one of Eunice's colleagues telling Eunice that she should not encourage children to read fiction as it gave them too much imagination!

Colin McNaughton is an author and illustrator. Since leaving the Royal College of Art in 1975 he has worked exclusively in the colourful world of children's books. His picture books include *The Pirats*, published by Ernest Benn, *A Ship to Sail the Seven Seas*, published by Kestrel, and *Football Crazy* published by Heinemann. This book features the star of our item, *Rollerbear*, namely Bruno the Bear.

Spike Milligan is Spike Milligan, which says it all. He scribbles down his little poems for children whenever, and wherever, they spring into his mind. He then stuffs them into a drawer in his desk until a publisher persuades him that it is time he put them together into another book. He is the nearest thing we have in this country to a comic genius and every bookshop in the country—perhaps in the world—has his books.

Cynthia Mitchell has written two books of verse for children. They are *Halloweena Hecatee* and *Hop-Along Happily* and both are published by Heinemann. She is Deputy Head of an infants' school in Yorkshire and is well known for her writings on education.

Frank Muir has been known to appear on television and be heard on radio but he is really a writer who used to write scripts but now writes books. Readers who enjoyed our *What-a-Mess* item might like to know that the small, fat, scruffy Afghan puppy is the hero (hero?) of a series of five picture books published by Ernest Benn and, in paperback, Carousel.

Polly Muir is the wife of the above and this is the first book which they have worked on together. They found that their tastes were remarkably similar. Which is probably a good thing for peace in the home.

Jamie Muir works for an Arts programme on television. He is joint-author of a book on Christmas and its traditions. He also translated from the German a funny book supposed to tell all about the disastrously badly designed secret weapons of history, *Halbritter's Armoury*, published by Ernest Benn. This last was not an easy task as he does not speak German.

Sally Muir was in publishing but now designs and makes knitted things. She has edited a small book of poems, *Edward Thomas*, published by J.L. Carr. This is the first children's story written by her and illustrated by her brother Jamie.

Barbara Paterson has written more about Henny in *Henny Takes a Hand*, published by Hippo. She used to write for the magazine *Petticoat* and has produced an invaluable survival kit for young adults in *Help!*, published by Peacock.

Kate Penoyre studied at Bristol and Canterbury Colleges of Art. She lives in a cottage with a big garden in Sussex. Besides illustrating stories she is a graphic designer who has worked on greetings cards and book jackets and is also a landscape painter.

Sir Ralph Richardson is, of course, an actor, and one of the glories of our stage. He has a tremendously wide range of interests, including powerful motor-bikes, ferrets, a parrot and reading. He really did have a pug. This is the first story he has ever written for children.

Harry Secombe is one of our best loved comedians, a founder-Goon and a fine singer. He is also a writer, an activity which he enjoys more and more. His books include a funny novel *Twice Brightly*, published by Robson Books and Sphere Books; *Goon for Lunch*, published by Michael Joseph and Star Books, and his first book for children *Katy and the Nurgla*, published by Robson and Puffin (sequel on the way).

Jacqueline Sinclair has worked in advertising and for a design group as well as illustrating Barbara Paterson's *Yasmin and the Desert Snow*, and Patricia Cleveland-Peck's story collection, *The String Family*, both for Heinemann.

Agnes Szudek was born in Scotland but brought up in Northamptonshire. Her great ambition was to act but when she told her father he said "We don't do that in our family". So she didn't. And became a teacher. Her books are *Victoria Plumb*, *Victoria and the Parrots Gang* (her tomboy youth), *The Amber Mountain, Stories from Poland*, all published by Hutchinson, and *The Mighty Muddle* (the bedroom of one of her sons) which is published by Eel Pie.

John Thompson-Steinkrauss has a passionate interest in natural history, spending long hours in the countryside observing and drawing birds, animals and plants. He illustrated his first two books, *Rabbit* and *Black-Headed Gull*, published by Heinemann while still at art school.

Bill Tidy is perhaps our most prolific and successful cartoonist, with strip cartoons in a number of journals, e.g., *The Fosdyke Saga* in the *Daily Mirror*, *The Cloggies* in *Private Eye*, plus dozens of single cartoon drawings. He has illustrated many books, the most recent being Christopher Logue's *Book of Comic Verse*, published by Batsford. Our item, *Frankenstein Meets Spofforth Minor*, is the first strip cartoon he has drawn specially for children.

Ron and Atie van der Meer are Dutch, but live in England with their two little girls and write and illustrate picture books together. Ron also created *The Pop-Up Games Book* for Heinemann.

Martin Waddell lives at the foot of the Mountains of Mourne in Ireland. He writes ghost stories under the name of Catherine Sefton, published by Faber, and is producing a football series under his own name for Puffin. The first title is *Napper Goes for Goal*.

Robin and Jocelyn Wild have written and illustrated two books about Basher and his friends, *Spot's Dogs and the Alley Cats* and *Spot's Dogs and the Kidnappers*, both published by Heinemann. They live on a small-holding in Somerset with their two sons and a lot of animals, and are almost totally self-sufficient.

Peter Wingham studied illustration at the Royal College of Art and has since worked freelance. He has illustrated several books, among them his own picture book *The Toy Box* (Heinemann). He has a passion for motorbikes and comics.

Joseph Wright was born in Ulverston, as was Stan Laurel. He studied at the Royal College of Art where he was a student of Quentin Blake and his work has been seen in a great number of publications. He lives in London with his wife, who is a designer, and son Sam. *What-a-Mess* was the first picture book he illustrated.

John Yeoman is Head of the English Department at the French school in London, the Lycée. He gives as his hobbies "marking, and listening to the operas of Verdi". Most of his writing is done in collaboration with Quentin Blake and together they have produced some seven books.

If you would like to know more about any of our authors and illustrators, or their books, write to us:

Frank and Polly Muir
Heinemann Young Books
10 Upper Grosvenor Street
London W1X 9PA